The
Personhood
of God

The
Personhood
of God

Biblical Theology,
Human Faith
and the
Divine Image

Dr. Yochanan Muffs
Foreword by Dr. David Hartman

For People of All Faiths, All Backgrounds

JEWISH LIGHTS Publishing
Nashville, Tennessee

The Personhood of God:
Biblical Theology, Human Faith and the Divine Image
© 2005 by Yochanan Muffs
Foreword © 2005 by David Hartman
Preface © 2005 by Yocheved Herschlag Muffs

Library of Congress Cataloging-in-Publication Data
Muffs, Yochanan.
The personhood of God : biblical theology, human faith, and the divine image / Yochanan Muffs ; foreword by David Hartman.
    p. cm.
Includes bibliographical references and index.
ISBN 1-58023-265-5 (hardcover)
ISBN 978-1-58023-338-5 (paperback)
1. God—Biblical teaching. 2. Bible. O.T.—Criticism, interpretation, etc. 3. Bible. O.T.—Theology. 4. Image of God. 5. God (Judaism)
I. Title.
BS1192.6.M84 2005
296.3'11—dc22

                                                           2005014703

Manufactured in the United States of America
Cover Design: Tim Holtz
Cover Fabric Art: Yocheved Herschlag Muffs
Indexing: John Dibs

For People of All Faiths, All Backgrounds
Published by Jewish Lights Publishing
An Imprint of Turner Publishing Company
4507 Charlotte Avenue, Suite 100
Nashville, TN 37209
Tel: (615) 255-2665
www.jewishlights.com

To Yocheved

CONTENTS

CONTENTS

FOREWORD

DR. DAVID HARTMAN

I have known Yochanan Muffs for over forty years. He is my friend and the teacher who opened up the Bible for me as an exciting and engaging human-theological drama.

Yochanan Muffs, known throughout the world as one of the leading contemporary biblical scholars, is a biblical philologist and an expert in Mesopotamian religion and its influence on the Bible. Yet the Yochanan I know—the scholar-poet, the master of midrashic analysis whose rich theological imagination reveals the gripping realism of the biblical God and the intensity of God's relationship to human history—is less known to the reading public.

As a reader of this book, you have the rare privilege of sharing in Yochanan's fascinating mode of imaginative exegesis and of gaining a new perspective on the theological dimension of the biblical narrative and worldview.

For many years I was influenced by Maimonides' philosophical approach to the Bible and his methodical attempts at removing by reinterpretation the embarrassment of the Bible's bold anthropomorphic presentation of God. Maimonides, a thinker rooted in the Aristotelian philosophic tradition, accepted as evident the necessary connection between change and imperfection and between emotions and the absence of freedom. His philosophic, religious concern was to articulate an approach to biblical language that would preserve the purity of what he believed was the demonstrably true conception of the divine reality.

In sharp contrast to Maimonides and other scholars' attempts at demythologizing the Bible, Yochanan Muffs unapologetically restores the vitality of the personhood of God. God's "humanity" is presented with such vivid and compelling realism that readers may experience difficulty in continuing to worship the impersonal God of the philosophers, preferring instead the full-bodied, "human" God of the Bible as seen through the eyes of Yochanan Muffs.

Maimonides' *Guide of the Perplexed* guides us in the struggle against idolatry and false conceptions of God. Yochanan Muffs guides us in the struggle against indifference and apathy in religious life. In contrast to the medievalist's aversion to ascribing passions and change to God lest they compromise the idea of divine perfection, Yochanan Muffs feels there is no shame or dishonor in presenting God as a young and impetuous persona who develops through mistakes, who ultimately matures— with the help and intervention of prophetic partners—into a divine lover who expresses the deep yearning for a loving relationship with the people of Israel.

God is not a static, unchanging reality, but a dynamic, evolving *person* actively interacting with human beings in history and with His beloved community, Israel. Here there is no leap to a transcendent God but rather a leap into one's own psychic life where the humanity of God can be understood and, at times, emulated.

I am grateful to Jewish Lights for recognizing the importance of publishing Yochanan's incomparable work of biblical exegesis. This book offers not only a key to reading the Bible and understanding God in a new way, but also to encountering a refreshing and open approach to Judaism, one that does not thrive on the negation of the secular world or of unfamiliar patterns of thought. In presenting the most authoritative text of our tradition in a new way, this work of biblical exegesis shows us that Judaism can be strengthened and revitalized by interacting with the intellectual and experiential opportunities of the modern world.

Thank you, Yochanan, for being my teacher and the teacher of the people of Israel. You have helped us understand that only in embracing our own humanity and the psychological dynamics of the human condition will we be able to meet the God of the Bible.

PREFACE

A psychologically oriented, mythically formulated phenomenology of the world-affirming God as He appears
in the Bible and in later rabbinic traditions would be
valuable to those theists, atheists, and agnostics who
cultivate humanistic values. Since the phenomenology
can be accepted either as a psychological poem or as a
reflection of some ontological reality, it may possibly
serve as the basis of faith which humanist of all kinds
can hold in common.

—from Chapter 21

The Personhood of God is a reflection and an outgrowth of the
ideas expressed in the statement above. A major concern of
Yochanan Muffs, both as a teacher and as a scholar, is the relationship between the civilization of the ancient Near East and
the Hebrew Bible. Specifically, his interests are two interrelated
phases of these cultures: laws and mythical statements about
their anthropomorphic gods.

His previous works, *Studies in the Aramaic Legal Papyri
from Elephantine* (1969) and *Love & Joy: Laws, Language and*

Religion in Ancient Israel (1992), were devoted to the illumination of the continuity of legal terminology in the Near East, from Mesopotamia to the Talmud. The mode of analysis was philological-psychological. By means of a philological treatment of key terms, he determined the underlying psychology of certain transactions, such as *sale* and *gift*. His studies of ancient Near Eastern legal formulae were a necessary prelude to his study of biblical religion.

The first two parts of this book, "Biblical God in Relationship with a People" and "The Divine Person," present historical and phenomenological investigations of the anthropomorphic myths of the Near East. They especially emphasize the character of YHWH, who, although different from the gods of Mesopotamia in His nonidentity with nature, is nevertheless conceived of and experienced as a *person* with a will and a character that expresses itself dramatically in myth. The nature of this personality—with its imperfections, and perhaps even amorality—has been an embarrassment to those who like to think their abstract notions of divinity are rooted in the Bible.

The third part, "Aesthetic Sensibility and Religious Imagination," may seem to be extraneous to believing readers and students of religion. But, as Muffs puts it, "the aesthetic experience ... is much more than a hedonistic love of pleasure; it is also an attempt to relate the transcendent and the spiritual to the immediate and the libidinal" (page 103). Thus, aesthetics is not an added luxury, but an essential component of human personhood.

The fourth part, "Joy, Love, and Liturgy," presents philological and psychological treatments of prayer in antiquity. The studies in this section explore the implications of terms for devotion and willingness in rabbinic prayer. Thus, the term *love* "is the opposite of fear, not only metaphysically, but also legally and ritually" (page 149). These terms were so much a part of the literary atmosphere of the ancient Near East that they found their way into not only Jewish prayer, but also the liturgies of several Eastern churches.

The final part, "Encountering the Personhood of God," brings us to the concerns of the contemporary world. Here Muffs explores the painful but often creative conflict between religion and the world, the holy and the profane, the spiritual order and secular culture.

ACKNOWLEDGMENTS

It has been my privilege to edit this book by my husband, Professor Yochanan Muffs. The essays collected in this volume present Muffs's endeavor to explore the essence of biblical religion and the personhood of God. Most of them were written in the 1960s and early 1970s, and are set in the context of the biblical scholarship of that period.

Earlier versions of some of these essays were given to his students and colleagues. One of the scholars who has been familiar with Yochanan's work for decades is Dr. David Hartman, director of the Shalom Hartman Institute in Jerusalem.

In 1998, Dr. Hartman invited Yochanan to present many of these essays to a seminar of Senior Fellows, where they were discussed with great enthusiasm. We are thankful for his continuing encouragement.

Dr. Michael Swirsky, one of the participants in the seminar, suggested they become the basis for a book. He generously developed a structure and did the initial editing. Without his help, there would have been no book.

Back in the United States, Elisheva Urbas continued the editing process, ever diligent about maintaining Yochanan's voice.

Dr. Diane Sharon, friend, former student and colleague, was always available for consulting on scholarly and editorial issues. Hers was a labor of love—and invaluable.

Job Jindo, Yochanan's student, prepared the endnotes, checked sources, and reviewed the manuscript in its various stages. His help, his devotion, and his kindness have been incalculable.

Finally, many thanks to Berhanu Yosef, Benin Nefesh, and Philip Sadeh, who helped in a myriad of ways. And many thanks to Alys Yablon and Sarah McBride of Jewish Lights for their first-rate editorial work on this book.

Yocheved Herschlag Muffs

INTRODUCTION

MONOTHEISM, ANTHROPOMORPHISM, AND

THE PERSONHOOD OF GOD

The anthropomorphic depiction of God in the Bible has been a delight to midrashists and mystics on the one hand, and an outrage to philosophers and theologians on the other. Philosophers have been offended by the immorality of the image presented and by the attribution of human qualities such as form and personality to the ultimate principle. But not only have the naive pious felt no shame in God's so-called humanity, they have even seen in it His very glory. He is not an abstract principle but a real personality involved in the human situation. Both Christians and Jews, each in their own way, have even accepted God's physical attributes without much care. Some Jewish mystics delighted in the sight of the divine *soma* (literally "body") and Christians always considered the incarnation as *the* symbol of God's involvement in the world. New Testament Christianity went so far in its somatization of the Divine that God's psychic qualities were often attenuated, or, in the case of certain Jewish mystics, the attribution of sexuality to the Divine often resulted in outbreaks of religious nihilism in the social sphere. Prephilosophical Jews and Christians accepted both psychic and somatic anthropomorphism as a root principle of their faith.[1]

1

Most modern theologies—Jewish, Christian, or Muslim—on the other hand, simply adjust the old anthropomorphic traditions to some of the demands of philosophy: God is still a person, but this personhood has been stripped of all somatic content. God, in all three faiths, has been reduced—or elevated, according to one's own personal taste—to an impersonal principle: Omniscient, Omnipotent, All-Good, Infinite, and so on. The interpersonal drama—with its tension, absurdity, and humor—has been read away for the sake of doctrinal propriety. Thus, neither philosophy nor myth has had its way: in fact, both have had their wings clipped. Philosophy has lost its radical doubt (God is still affirmed as a person), while myth has lost its fire (God is not much of a person).

Since the Bible records the dramatic story of God's relationship to Israel, it is more than unfortunate that this central theme was not treated according to its own inner logic: literarily or dramatically. Any drama is a clash between personae. To understand the drama is to understand the personalities of the actors. Thus, any good literary critic must be an intuitive psychologist. By psychology, I do not mean a specific analytic school, but the intuitive understanding of human character, the wisdom and common sense about human affairs that all wise men—especially novelists and poets—have always possessed, even millennia before Freud. Thus, to understand the nature of the drama we must penetrate the psychology of the actors. Since their personalities are made articulate by their words and actions and are not always clearly spelled out, a certain amount of reading between the lines is needed—that is, reading through the lines and not arbitrarily creating new ones.

Most modern studies of religion start with man: man's attitude toward God, toward the world, toward himself. This is certainly the proper orientation for a modern theology, but not necessarily for a phenomenology of biblical religion where, according to the simple meaning of the text, God is more important than man: it is He who initiates the process of creation, He who summons man and enters into a covenant relationship with him, and so on. Therefore, in our study of the biblical record, the person of God—rather than of man—is our central concern.

The use of terms like *immanent* and *transcendent* often serve to obfuscate the problem: God clearly is not as much of this world as the term *immanent* would suggest, nor is He as out of the world as the term *transcendent* might indicate. God is both close and far. Even though He is not close in the sense that He is identified with the world, derived from it, or subject to it, He is intensely concerned with the people who live in the world, specifically with Israel. There is no doubt that God appears in the Bible as a person possessed with a wide range of emotions: concern, joy, sadness, regret, and chagrin, among many others.

In the various Mesopotamian texts, there is a tendency to subsume all of the gods and their respective functions and to concentrate them in a single high god. Thus, for example, Enlil was the high god: Shamash the sun god would be his eyes, Ishtar his hands, Ea his legs, and so forth down the line. It is a kind of mystical monotheism that can be compared with the Jewish mystical doctrine of *Adam Qadmon* (the first man). God is depicted in the form of the human body and His various moral attributes—mercy, justice, truth, glory, splendor—are associated with different organs of His body. God, expressed by the living organism of *Adam Qadmon*, was a creature of the whole reign of moods, potencies, and powers.

In some way, these models shed light on the relationship of biblical religion, at least as it was depicted by the Bible, to Mesopotamian civilization. YHWH, the One God, may have abolished all contenders and ruled alone, but He did not get rid of their various functions (attributes) by which the cosmos was run. The natural order had to go on. The heavens had to be provided with rain, the earth and mankind had to be nourished, children had to be gestated if they were to come into being. Man had to be provided for from birth to old age and even beyond.

Since there was only One God now, He necessarily had to take over all—and I emphasize the word *all*—of the powers, functions, and obligations of the old multidietied pantheon. Since He was a fusion and concentration of all the old powers, He could perform these functions with a sublime ease and facility never seen before. Or so He argued with His hardheaded constituency, Israel.

He was a whole pantheon in Himself. He was not only God the father, God the husband, the king and ultimate master but also God the spice maker, architect, interior decorator of the *mishkan* (Tabernacle), artist. God the teacher, God the scribe; God the gynecologist, God the midwife, God the veterinarian. God the creditor, God the debtor, God the playwright, God the sublime chess player who delights in playing moral games with His son, man, created in His image. God occasionally laughed and more often cried; He was consoled by prophets, and His anger was cooled by prophets and zealots. He walked, rested, and slept, but He was always awake. God wore a cap and a suit of clothes He called Israel; His hands were tattooed with the same name. He wore phylacteries in which were written the words "Who is like My people Israel, the one unique people in the land?"

God was a king who in His youth behaved in one way and in His older age, poetically speaking, yet another. Having learned from His mistakes, He now allowed His mercy—His underlying love for man (His creature, student, and collaborator)—to overcome His anger. God could be worshipped by man since He was so much like him. He constantly appeared in many and ever-changing roles lest He be frozen and converted into the dumb idols He Himself despised. God was a polyvalent personality who, by mirroring to man His many faces, provided the models that man so needed to survive and flourish.

This is the true humanity of God.

A NOTE ON THE TRANSLATION

The translation of the Hebrew Bible is primarily from the Jewish Publication Society's translation of *The Tanakh* (1985). In some instances, the translations are my own. The debate about gender and God language is ongoing. In the interest of simplicity, and to preserve the essence of original texts in Hebrew as well as other ancient Near Eastern languages, I have used the male form. Similarly, throughout the centuries, the Rabbis (rabbinic scholars of the first several centuries CE) spoke of "man" as including all humankind, male and female both. I have chosen to continue that tradition as well.

A NOTE ON THE TRANSLITERATION

I have adopted a popular system for transliteration of Hebrew, except for the following letters, which have no English equivalent:

alef = '
het = ḥ (pronounced as the guttural "ch" in German)
tet = ṭ
khaf = kh (pronounced as the guttural "ch" in German)
ayin = ʻ
tsade = ṣ

For transliteration of other Semitic languages, the following letters and diacriticals are often used: ḫ for velar *het* and š for *shin*.

Part I

THE BIBLICAL GOD
IN RELATIONSHIP
WITH A PEOPLE

One

PAGANISM AND BIBLICAL RELIGION

No religion is like any other. Each represents a unique world of thought. But religions do not exist in isolation; they are connected to one another in many ways. Take, for example, the intimate relationship between the religion of the Patriarchs and the religions of Sumer, Babylonia, and Assyria. Here the skeptics protest: "Stop distorting the Scriptures! Stop reading into them what is not there! There never was any such a connection!" Yet Scripture itself testifies to an interconnection: "Your ancestors lived in Mesopotamia: Terah, the father of Abraham, the father of Nahor. And they worshipped foreign gods" (Josh. 24:2).

The Israelite mode of relating to other religions was one of creative absorption. This is proven by the fact that certain legal patterns appear only in the Bible and in the much earlier Nuzi documents, indicating a clear line of influence.[1] But in spite of the deep-rootedness of Abraham and the other Israelite patriarchs in the soil of the ancient Near East, as soon as Abraham heard the earthshaking call to "Go forth from your land, from your homeland, from the house of your father"(Gen. 12:1), he rejected all the heavenly science, all the marvelous literature, and all the esoteric theosophy of the Babylonians.

Abraham got up and left, and the echoes of this revolutionary exodus are still reverberating in the world today.[2]

This rootedness of Abraham in the wider Near Eastern culture and his sudden break with it are telling symbols of the ambivalent relationship of Israel to its environment: a willingness to borrow external forms, on the one hand, and an almost total rejection of their spiritual content, on the other. The Rabbis depict beautifully the revolutionary character of Abrahamic religion, for example, in the legend that has Abraham smashing the idols in his father's shop.

One must be careful not to take this story too literally; after all, Babylonia of those days was the center of a great culture, and its religion was much richer and deeper than the unenlightened worship of statues. Anyone who would like to penetrate into the inner spirit of Judaism had better get to know the religious life of Terah, the father of Abraham the rebel. Such penetration is possible for our generation more than for any preceding it because it is in our day that archeology has pried open the closed gates of the ancient Babylonian world of thought.

UMBILICUS MUNDI

One of the most important archeological finds is the Babylonian creation epic, the *Enuma Elish*. This epic tells of how, in the beginning, there existed only the primordial waters, symbolized by the dragon goddess, Tiamat. But this primordial world did not lie inert; rather, it was like a big pot of soup, bubbling with the seeds of future generations. These generations emerged youthful and throbbing with virility. Their raucous enthusiasm disturbed the sleep of the older gods, whose leader was Tiamat. We know how youngsters can sometimes deprive their elders of their afternoon siesta. This myth, however, is not about old folks and young folks, but about the tension between creativity and stasis. The moral is: You cannot suppress creativity very long.

Tiamat gets herself elected leader of the group and goes out with her army to destroy the young rebels, who have killed her husband, Kingu, and who continue to disturb the sleep of the older gods. At first they prove too much for her, and a great fear falls on the elders. They gather together in council to devise a strategy for dealing with the revolution. The rebels are led by the temporary dictator, the youngest god of all, Marduk. Marduk girds his loins and arms himself with the latest weaponry in order to ensure his success in battle. He wears a red paste on his lips, a type of good-luck charm, a magical *kame'a* (amulet). Marduk conquers the monster goddess Tiamat and splits her body into two parts. From her upper part, he forms the *raqi'a,* the "heavens," and from the lower part he forms the earth.

Up to now, the role of man has not been mentioned. But the story is not yet finished. The Babylonian gods, like those of the Greeks, were slaves to all sorts of physical needs. The nectar and ambrosia of the Olympian gods were not mere poetry but a reality, for eating and drinking were divine needs. Without nourishment, the gods could not survive. Until now, the gods had to provide their own food. Now Marduk decreed that the gods of heaven would be relieved of this tiresome chore. In his wisdom, Marduk created man to be a slave to the gods, one who would provide divine nutriment. In short, we can say that man and human society were created specifically to free the gods from the necessity of feeding themselves.[3] Human society was like a tremendous plantation, where human beings were serfs and the king or high priest the overseer. The sacrifices the latter made from the produce of the serfs provided food for the gods, and the temple was a cosmic dining room. The gods were masters of the plantation.[4]

Later in the *Enuma Elish,* it is told that after the flood waters had receded from the earth, Utnapishtim (literally, "he who has found life"), the Babylonian Noah, went out of the ark and offered sacrifices. Immediately, the gods gathered around the altar "like hungry flies." Why such an uncontrollable hunger?

Because all during the flood, the sacrificial order had been disturbed, leaving the gods literally to starve to death.

THE NATURE OF IDOLATRY

The major characteristic of idolatry is not the number of gods but rather the dependence of the gods on a sphere of reality that transcends them. The gods do not have full control over their fates. They are born against their will; they die against their will. If they don't eat, they get hungry and weak, and ultimately they die. They are subject to internal, physical needs but also to external, magical forces. There is a mysterious power in substances, in forms, in numbers, and in colors. No god ever put it there; it is a given. Just as water is wet and fire hot, so certain substances are intrinsically powerful and dangerous. The power of magic is natural and autonomous. It is not dependent on the will of the gods. On the contrary, it is the gods who are dependent on it.

Not only are the gods subservient to natural impulses and magical powers; they are also subject to time. There are lucky times and there are unlucky times, those that are intrinsically evil and dangerous. Just as the gods did not introduce magical power into certain objects, so the gods did not create the good times and the bad times. Just as the gods are subject to magic, so are they subject to, and frightened by, the evil times. By way of summary, we can say that the subjugation of the gods to an independent, impersonal realm—that of nature, magic, and time—is characteristic of pagan religion everywhere, in all its manifestations. It is not the number of deities that is decisive: one god can be as subject to fate as a hundred gods. For example, Akhenaton worshipped one god who was subject to the rhythm of nature; he died every evening and was reborn every morning. Yehezkel Kaufmann calls this realm to which the gods are subject "the metadivine sphere."[5]

THE NATURE OF BIBLICAL RELIGION

Abraham came and broke the idols of Terah. Judaism appeared and brought about one of the great intellectual revolutions of all time. Judaism liberated divinity from all subjugation to a metadivine realm. The God of Israel is not a slave to nature or to matter; rather, He creates the world of nature by His sovereign will. God is not a slave to independent natural law; it is He who determines the laws of heaven and earth (Ps. 19). He does not contend with fate or time; rather, it is He who summons the generations in advance (Isa. 41:4). He was not born and will not die (Hab. 1:12). He does not sleep (Ps. 121); and He has no need of sacrifice and offerings (Ps. 50).[6]

And how does this personality, free of all limitation, express itself? By an act of turning, of interest, of love. But there are many kinds of love. That attributed to the Divine by Aristotle is essentially self-love. How can a being that is absolute, self-sufficient, eternal, and unchangeable love anyone or anything but itself? How can the perfect One become involved in an imperfect external world? Aristotle's god was doomed to eternal self-contemplation, because the perfect can contemplate only the perfect. Yet this is not so for the God of Israel. His personality finds its true expression in love for another personality, independent and outside itself. It is a great love that cannot be contained by the boundaries of the self, a love that seeks involvement of the divine heart with its human counterpart.

This is the secret of what Heschel called "God in search of man," for man is almost a divine need, created to be the partner of the divine love. Nothing expresses this relationship with greater clarity than biblical prophecy, the very center of which is divine concern with man.

INDIFFERENCE AND OMENS

One should not take this display of interest too lightly, for the true turning of God toward man was a total revolution in the religious world of the ancient Near East. The gods of Babylonia were completely dependent on nature and fate. Their major interest was themselves: the satisfaction of their needs, their hates, and their loves. The gods of Babylonia were not interested in the private destiny of man. To satisfy their physical needs, they turned only to the king, using a form of revelation similar to the messenger prophecy of Israel.[7] But the content of this appeal was limited to one thing: the gods' need for food. In the form of a dream, they would reveal to the king their urgent need to rebuild an ancient temple from its ruins and reinstate its sacrificial service. But they did not turn to Everyman at all. Therefore, the common people remained confused in their attempt to come to terms with everyday existence. They were anxious lest some action of theirs might not find favor in the eyes of the gods. Or perhaps a certain day might not be proper for investment or for marriage.

Because the gods did not reveal their will voluntarily, men had to struggle to find a way to it, so that they could, so to speak, take the temperature of the gods. This method is known as omenology. The Babylonians believed that the feelings of the gods reflected themselves in natural manifestations. Every natural event—an eclipse of the sun, an earthquake, the position of the stars and planets, a defect in a human fetus, an imperfection in the liver of an animal—tells us something important about the mood of the divinity. These phenomena were thought to mirror divine anger and joy. But the mirror was not clear. The language of the omens was symbolic. It needed an exegesis. And only a priest who was an expert in the exegesis of omenology knew how to decipher the secrets of this Babylonian Torah. Interpretation of omens was a type of science based on empirical observation and on the necessary causal relationship between natural phenomena and human life. For example, if on the second day of Kislev at three in the afternoon, at a particular confluence of planets, the king left his house and fell into a pit, there must be a scientific connection between the day, the position of the planets, and the accident of the king. Therefore, let the king be very careful next year not to go out at that hour, for the accident might just repeat itself.

This complicated, scientific *"torah"* sprang from the existential anguish of human beings who suffered from divine indifference and needed some way of discerning the divine mood. One can characterize the religion of the pagans as "man in search of god."

LOVE AND PROPHECY

In Israel, man does not have to search for God, for He is constantly searching for man. What need is there for omens when, generation after generation, God repeatedly tries to make His will known to His people? What need is there for a human science to crack the omens if there exists a permanent institution of dialogue?[8] If there is visual symbolism in biblical prophecy, it is nothing but an aid to understanding a clear preceding message. The symbolism is not the prophecy itself; prophecy spelled out does not need interpretation. And if the prophets occasionally garnish their prophecies with a sign, like the almond branch and the seething pot of Jeremiah (1:11–19), this realistic concretization serves only to lend additional clarity to an otherwise explicit message. What is more, it is not a learned doctor of omenology who cracks the code of this symbolism, but YHWH Himself, in an unequivocal manner. And if you happen to find Joseph interpreting omens at the court of Pharaoh, it is only to show that it is YHWH who runs the show:[9] "So Joseph said to them, 'Surely God can interpret! Tell me [your dreams]'" (Gen. 40:8). "And Pharaoh said to Joseph, 'I have had a dream, but no one can interpret it. Now I have heard it said of you that for you to hear a dream is to tell its meaning.' Joseph answered Pharaoh, saying, 'Not I! God will see to Pharaoh's welfare'" (Gen. 41:15–16). Not only is omenology not the characteristic mode of Divine-human interconnection; there is no omenology in Israel, no divination in Jacob. And if Jews on occasion interpret prophetic symbolism for Gentile kings, this act of interpretation comes to teach us that it is YHWH who is the master of history, the ultimate and final interpreter of natural phenomena.

The Babylonians were a people of omens and Israel a people of prophetic revelation. The nations of the world desperately sought ways of penetrating the fog surrounding the divine realm. Only an expert in the secrets of existence, in the science of gnosis or philosophy, knew the road. Not so with Israel, whose God Himself opened a road to man to converse with him, to reveal to him His will and the secrets of His heart in a language that would be intelligible to every man. Biblical prophecy is the bridge of conversation that enables the intimate meeting between the divine personality and its human counterpart to take place.

LEAP OF ACTION

Any meeting of personalities requires great bravery. One who attempts to communicate with another endangers his own life, for to do this he must reveal what is in his heart. Such an act is potentially dangerous because one does not know ahead of time if he will find a receptive ear. There is always the possibility that the ear of the listener will be impervious. Any real communication, then, is a dangerous leap. But if one never screws up the courage to jump, he will wither away in silent isolation. There are two choices: to love or to die. One can hardly conceive of a death more tragic than that caused by a love that does not find its destined partner.

The Holy One, blessed be He, took a great chance when, at Sinai, He spoke with Israel for the first time. This act of communication was also an act of love. But God did not know ahead of time, so to speak, if His intended bride would be responsive to His voice: "I only hope their hearts will always be as responsive, as willing to obey Me, as they were just now" (Deut. 5:26). How much anxiety is wrapped up in these awful words. And in fact their ears did prove insensitive. Generation after generation, Israel strayed from God.

But so great was His love, He repeatedly sent messengers to renew the bonds that had weakened. The messengers were the prophets of Israel, who cried, morning, noon, and night, "Repent, O backsliding sons. I shall cure your lack of faith" (Jer. 3:22) and "Arm yourself with words and repent" (Hos. 14:3). Yet Israel did not pay attention to the voice of the prophets until God came personally to renew the marriage contract. "I made myself available, even though they did not request it from me. I said, 'Here I am, Here I am.' I stretched out my hands all day long to a rebellious people, who walk on a wicked path after the machinations of their heart" (Isa. 55: 1–2).

This dialectical tension in the loving relationship—the painful need to express feeling and the anxiety that the expression might not be properly received—is the inner dialectic of the human personality, as well as of the Divine, and is impossible to avoid. Mankind can only overcome this tension by imitating God Himself, by undertaking an act of bravery, a leap of faith, as God has done—by reaching out to the other, to communicate, to love.

Two

THE ESSENCE OF BIBLICAL PROCESS

In its essence, the biblical process is a concerted movement away from the magical, impersonal, and mechanical and toward the direction of greater "personalness." Nature and its immanent laws are no longer the focus of ultimate concern. At the same time, while nature is emptied of its divinity, it is never denied or denigrated. Instead, it becomes the stage on which personhood works out its own destiny. Freedom and responsibility, interpersonal love and betrayal, anger and hate now become the root metaphors of religious thinking. Man is in control of his own destiny, using his freedom not to control the outer physical reality in a manipulative, scientific fashion, but rather to enter into a loving dialogue with God and his fellow man, against the backdrop of a divinely created world. This seems to be the essential theme of the literature of the Bible as a whole.

Nature is to be used and enjoyed; it is neither an end in itself nor a mere burden or impediment to ultimate perfection. There is no bemoaning the transience of natural phenomena or yearning for an unchanging essence beyond being and becoming. Nature is the creation of the only unchanging being, nature's transience but a reflection of its creatureliness—an

19

attribute it shares with man. If nature has any permanence, it is not inherent but part of a divine plan.

To the Greeks and the people of India, nature is the ultimate reality. Its essence is its constancy, its adherence to eternal, inherent laws. Nature is the regular, the unchanging, the determined. In the fullest sense, even personality cannot function without the firm substratum of nature, of which it is a part. Hence, while nature is in this sense only secondary, ancillary to the activities of the personality, it is never denigrated.[1]

Once again, let us stress this basic point: any study of paganism that centers its attention on the number of gods in the pantheon is being misled by a biblical prejudice, passed on through the Judeo-Christian tradition, which understands the difference between biblical religion and paganism in numerical terms. From a pagan point of view, the gods and their number are not the ultimate sphere of interest. What came before the gods and what will remain after their demise is the ultimate concern of pagan religion. This is the view of Greek classicist Frances Cornford and biblical scholar Yehezkel Kaufmann.[2]

FREEDOM OF RELATION

Personality cannot function without freedom. But such freedom can take several different directions. Man can be free in his attempt to transcend the natural process and its servitude; this is the religious freedom of the mystic and the Buddhist. Even where there are ordained cycles of being, the great man may, through knowledge, escape his fate and hasten his liberation from the web of terrestrial existence. Man can also direct his freedom toward nature, in an attempt to master it and subject it to his will. This is the freedom of the scientist. In each case freedom is completely independent and self-centered. However, there is a third use of freedom: to communicate and relate to another person. Without the ability to overcome fear and inhibition and without the necessary control over one's self, this communicative expression of self is impossible. It is the freedom of relatedness that is celebrated by the Bible, not the competitive freedom of virtuosity but the cooperative freedom of dialogue.

The first use of freedom is an attempt to disengage oneself from the world. The second is an attempt to control the world. The third is an attempt to be human by relating to other human beings. The Bible is not a mystical document; it is not so involved with the world as to need liberation from it. Nor is it a scientific book.

The religion of the Bible is not an outgrowth of polytheism, as some maintain. In most polytheistic religions, there is a sphere of natural reality beyond the gods. The more sophisticated forms of pagan religion do not merely unify their pantheons but demythologize them. What they are left with is nature and its laws. Nature is conceived of either as spirit (and the principle of motion) or matter. The latter view leads directly into science, the former into mysticism. None leads to the interpersonal, because the metadivine is never conceived of as personal. On the contrary, the personal gods are nothing but crude personifications of natural processes.

Assuming that the Bible derives developmentally from preexisting Near Eastern paganism, why does it not develop further, into either science or mysticism, the ultimate concerns of which are nature? Such a development would not be problematical or radical, since all pagan religions know a period before the gods were personalized. Sophisticated paganism merely returns to the primal objects of religious interest, which were never entirely superseded by the reign of the personalized gods. What happens in Israel is most unexpected. It is as if the personalized gods win out, are fused into one, and defeat nature, *dharma* and *moira* (approximately, "fate" and "cosmic law").

ISRAEL AND THE PROCESS OF PERSONALIZATION

In paganism, the primordial reality is impersonal fate, which then becomes progressively personalized, first in the form of a diffuse and undefined daimon, then in the form of a god. Science reverses the direction of personalization by removing the personal gods and going back to the primitive, undifferentiated, impersonal ground of being. Pagan religion never successfully resolves the tension between impersonal fate *(moira, ananke)* and the personal gods; the two always remain in tension with each other. Although in the Near East, and especially in Mesopotamia, daimonism is transcended and the personalities of the gods are clearly delineated (unlike in Egypt, where they and the divine kings are pale shadows without any personal color), they become so aloof and Apollonian that they lose their human significance and can easily be deposed. The *ṭuppi-šīmāti* (tablets of destiny) are stolen, and the gods nearly perish. Then and only then can nature reassert herself. Personhood is thus conquered by nature and science because the personalities of the gods are not powerful enough to resist them.

In Israel, on the other hand, the process of personalization continues on to a higher stage. The divine personality, instead of becoming silly or pallid, as it does in Greece and India, becomes so strong that it is seen to dominate nature, which is then no longer perceived as a preexistent reality but as a product of the divine, personal will. While the Greeks, in their science, return to the more primitive *moira,* Israel progresses in the direction of personhood that the religious world has already been taking. In the human sense, Israel represents an advance, while Greece represents a regression.

Why personhood becomes so strong in Israel that it is able to conquer nature cannot be explained developmentally. Could the breakthrough of personhood have taken place somewhere else? Was it inevitable? These questions cannot be answered either. But if one assumes that personality is part of the built-in logic of the human mind, it was probably only a matter of time. To use Teilhard de Chardin's method, a new genus fans out experimentally in all possible variations. Each of the great religions of antiquity is one manifestation of the ideal, an experiment aimed at uncovering the truth about existence.[3] The genius of Israel's religion as opposed to the others is its focus on the idea of the personhood of God. This idea is psychologically inevitable, built into the human psyche. It is, if you will, revelation.

Why didn't the pagan gods develop more meaningful personalities? What would have happened if they had? Their personalization is essentially selfish and egotistical. They are interested only in the satisfaction of their own needs. They do not yet know the secret of positive relatedness; instead, they compete for power and join together in cooperative action only in times of cosmic crisis. Once the crisis has passed, the coalition dissolves, and the original fighting and competition return.

The unification of the pantheon does not automatically make the resulting divinity any less self-centered. Akhenaton's one god is not particularly concerned with the souls of human beings; if he has any relationship to humanity it is to the king and his immediate family alone. He is not the god of morality but the god of the sun. Aristotle's prime mover is the perfect example of divine disinterest and self-centeredness. Thus, the oneness of Israel's God does not explain His interpersonal orientation, or, consequently, His moral character.

Both human and divine society were moving in the direction of personhood, but it was essentially the personalness of *arête*, individual excellence on the field of battle and especially in games. The excellent man is the hero and the winner in individual competition, *homo ludens* par excellence. The gods also participate in this personalness of combat and gamesmanship. Such personhood cannot develop much further, since it does not need the other for love or communication but only as an antagonist and sparring partner. Only when personhood is defined in terms of a dialogical interrelation between two persons are new and creative dimensions opened up. If they are not, the old idea of the dominance of nature reasserts itself in new forms. The gods are removed as impotent and meaningless. Reality is reduced to nature. Nature, no longer personified, is reduced to either spirit or matter. In the materialistic view, the new man of excellence is the scientist, who conquers nature with his intellect. In the spiritual view, the ideal is the man of mystical excellence, who conquers nature-sub-one (the physical world) by transcending it in favor of nature-sub-two (the realm of the spirit). The old ideas of the game and of preexistent nature are retained.

Even the sexuality of the pagan gods is not necessarily interpersonal. The Apollonian does not like sex, and when he does have it, it is rather crude; for example, Zeus comes down as a bull. The Dionysians, too, are ambivalent about sex. They are either orgiastic (hardly interpersonal) or ascetic (bent on starving the libido). Sex is thus either frozen or polarized. As Cornford points out, Greek philosophy is the history of the Apollonization of the Dionysian. Aristotle's prime mover is the cool peak of this development. It is only in the Bible that sexuality and interpersonality are joined together. This is certainly one of the lasting contributions of the Bible to man's self-realization.

Since personhood is interpersonal, the person of God must have some sustained, external focus of interest. One focus of interest necessarily precludes many foci. Thus God chooses/loves/becomes involved with Israel. He does not destroy the nations of the world, but neither does He direct His affections toward them. The relationship with Israel, like any real relationship, is permanent and structured, with mutual responsibilities clearly defined. Nonfulfillment of these terms brings anger and disappointment. Anger is not hidden; this would be dangerous, since hidden anger grows stronger and ultimately destroys the relationship. Rather, by venting the anger in reproach and criticism, it is cooled and relieved. Anger and its resolution, reproach, are not one sided. God gets angry at Israel and reproaches them by means of His prophets—but the people of Israel also get angry, when God does not seem to keep up His end of the relational bargain.[4]

The pagans do not know of a constant relationship of interpersonality initiated by a god with a whole human community, a relationship structured by mutual stipulation and sealed by a contract and an oath, a relationship established through the mediation of a prophet who transmits both divine love and divine anger. This combination of elements is unique to biblical Israel. Each one of the elements is profoundly evocative. For example, a pagan god might single out a particular king for his favor—ordinary human beings are beyond the pale of divine intimacy—but the relationship is tenuous at best, and there is no guarantee that the god's grace will be transferred to the king's heirs. Divine relationships are subject to the same instability (chaos) that constantly threatens the stability of both human relationships and of the cosmos as a whole. Indeed, in the Mesopotamian view, everything, with the exception of human law, is unstable.

THE TORAH AS A MEANS OF RELATIONSHIP

In Israel the relationship between God and man is stably structured and sealed by law and oath. It is eternal, for all subsequent generations are included in it. Moreover, it is a relationship not only with a king who can be adorned with titles of pseudodivinity (thus keeping the love more or less "within the family"), but with every member of the people. Thus, while broadly inclusive, the relationship remains a personal one, for it entails a contract with each individual separately. As Kaufmann has pointed out, the laws of the Torah are formulated in the second person singular (a point also noted by Walter Eichrodt).[5] This democracy of concern is certainly noteworthy. Man *qua* man now becomes the focus of permanent divine interest.

Even when the pagan gods take an interest in the lives of individual kings, the demands imposed on the latter are essentially cultic. The god promises the king long life and success if he takes good care of the god's temple and cult. This is probably the most important single responsibility of the king, more important than his secular administrative duties. I do not know whether kings were ever deposed for moral faults, but this is hardly the conclusion to be drawn from Hans Güterbock's study of Near Eastern historiography.[6] There, it is the cultic faux pas that causes the downfall of kings and dynasties alike. The cultic demand is hardly a deep or moral one: it is merely mechanical and selfish.

The essential demand of the God of Israel, on the other hand, is not cultic. Rather, the biblical God demands moral behavior from His people. As the prophets stress to the point of exaggeration, the cultic demands that are made on the wilderness generation are quite meager. Most of the sacrifices instituted are related to individual transgressions. Nowhere in the Bible do we find the austere anxiety that we find in Mesopotamia in connection with the erection of temples. However, the Bible is replete with exhortations to moral behavior, rather than to cultic performance. As Isaiah proclaims in the name of God, Israel is to do what is right and not abandon the righteous commandments of God. God explicitly rejects cultic performance in favor of social justice:

> Is this the fast I desire,
> A day for men to starve their bodies?
> Is it bowing the head like a bulrush
> And lying in sackcloth and ashes?
> Do you call that a fast,
> A day when YHWH is favorable?
> No, this is the fast I desire:
> To unlock the fetters of wickedness,
> And untie the cords of the yoke

To let the oppressed go free;
To break off every yoke.
It is to share your bread with the hungry,
And to take the wretched poor into your home;
When you see the naked, to clothe him,
And not to ignore your own kin. (Isa. 58:5–7)

Three

THEOLOGICAL ANTHROPOMORPHISM

Another way of characterizing the essence of the biblical world-view has to do with the use of anthropomorphism as a way of imagining the Divine. There are different kinds of theological anthropomorphism, depending on the concept of the anthropos, with each theology in reality reflecting a different anthropology. The anthropomorphism of the Babylonians is radically different from that of the Bible. From one point of view, the Babylonian gods, like the Apollonian gods of the Greek Olympus, are more "divine." Propriety prevents them from too intimate an involvement in human society, for they are essentially born aristocrats, modeled after the people who created them. But if the Greek and Babylonian gods are aristocrats, the God of Israel is, in many respects, a democrat, for He is friendly not only with kings but with commoners. The individuals He "adopts" are not only those of royal blood; He is ready to adopt and even "marry" an entire people of former slaves and to promise them a rich patrimony that He must then win for them in battle. To top all this, He goes so far as to enter into a contractual relationship with this people, using the magical-legal formulae and procedures that were commonly—this word is to be emphasized—used to bind nations.

The idea seems even more blasphemous when we consider the self-cursing nature of these contracts. From both the Bar Gayah and Mari inscriptions, we know that at covenantal ceremonies animals were cut into pieces, and from Jeremiah 34:8–22 we know that the parties then passed between the pieces. From Bar Gayah we know the significance of this "passing through": the contracting party was actually placing a curse on himself, such that if he broke the contract he would be cut up by the gods like this sacrificial animal. It is clear from the description of the contract between Abram and God in Genesis 15 that a symbolic surrogate of God Himself, the lapid of fire, passes between the pieces of the slaughtered animals. God is thus subjecting Himself to the same curse as the human participant! One cannot go much further anthropomorphically.

THE "HUMAN" GOD

To be sure, the pagan deities are not always superhuman. There are also those gods who are less human than mortals, sometimes to the point of causing embarrassment to them. Here the humanness of the biblical God is, by contrast, a sign of His superiority. In spite of some godlike excesses (most unbecoming a bourgeois divinity), this anthropomorphic deity is, on the whole, a paragon of human virtue, a kind of *Übermensch*, in comparison with the *urmensch* represented by the second type of pagan anthropomorphism. As we have shown, God's adoption of Israel and His entering into a covenantal relationship with them are certainly illustrations of His more human character. Another illustration is provided by His anger, which is of the kind that arises from betrayal by a loved one. Such anger, seemingly so unfitting for the Divine, is the very stamp of human dignity.

Let us also remember that the relationship between God

and Israel, according to the Priestly Code, is one of adoption, the formulae of which closely parallel actual Mesopotamian practice. If the adopted child is unfaithful, he is, according to Mesopotamian law, to be either killed, branded, or sold into slavery. The terms of the adoption of Israel are much more lenient; it can never be revoked, no matter how unfaithful the adoptee. And unfaithful the Israelites certainly are; they themselves record their own long history of defections. Though at times He seems on the point of annulling the contract and fulfilling His promises through the seed of Moses alone (Exod. 32:10), God never actually abandons His people, for, legally speaking, He has bound Himself to them for eternity.

Why does God always express His anger first to Abraham or Moses? Why does He not immediately act? According to Ezekiel (22:23–31), God actually wants the prophets to oppose His angry plans. In any case, the prophets are quite successful in staving off divine punishment. If God were as angry as He maintains, Moses's intercession could hardly succeed. As we see elsewhere, the divine anger can also be cooled, not only by the psychotherapy of intercession, but also by the medical method of inoculation. God's anger is like a pot ready to burst if some of the excess steam is not let off. Phinehas is "angry for YHWH" and kills the fornicating Midianite, but this release, by human means, of a small amount of the divine anger is enough to prevent it from exploding full force (Num. 25). If inoculation doesn't work, the soporific and intoxicating effect of incense can also be relied upon. This is not the domain of the prophet and his word, or of the zealot with his microtheistic anger, but of the priest with his censer.

This type of anthropomorphism would have been considered outrageous by all Mesopotamian pagans of orthodox learning. In their view, prophets cannot intercede because no human being stands close enough to the gods or has sufficient credit with them to be able to invoke their favor on someone else's behalf. Even kings cannot really intercede. All they can do in the hour of crisis is to offer themselves as magical fetishes or surrogate victims in order to placate the divine anger. They cannot intercede for another reason: prayer of the biblical sort implies an element of reasonableness that the pagan gods do not possess. The biblical prophet can argue using all the rational paraphernalia of a lawyer—including the same bad legal logic and appeals to the vanity of the judge. An argument is possible because God operates on more or less rational principles; He is not arbitrary but acts according to the laws of morality. If He punishes someone, the latter has a right to ask for justification. Like Job, he may not get it, but he is never punished for asking. The pagan king, on the other hand, cannot argue logically, since the god's actions might not have been for any good reason. What is more, the god to whom he is praying may not even have been the one who brought about the evil; it might have been some other god or, possibly, an independent demon or cosmic force. In fact, the only one who can actually intercede in Mesopotamian religion is neither a king nor a saint but a minor deity who, as one of the family, can approach the great gods whose actions affected human life.

As for the inoculation method, the idea that a human being can relieve the anger of a god by independently acting on his behalf is pure blasphemy in anybody's book, Jewish or pagan. That is certainly why no Jew ever quite understood what the passage in Ezekiel 22:23–31 actually meant. The only time a human acts on behalf of a Mesopotamian god is at the Akitu festival, where the king acts out the role of Marduk the Valiant and subsequently enters into a *hieros gamos,* a "sacred marriage," with a temple prostitute. This is hardly independent action; when he performs this ceremony, the king "is the god," appointed by the god himself and not self-delegated. Phinehas, in his vengeful zeal, champions God's cause on his own initiative. God even thanks him for it, rewarding him with the Royal Peace Medal (Num. 25:12) for otherwise He would have gotten out of control and destroyed Israel, something He evidently does not want to do. Yet Aaron's use of incense (Num. 17:12)—even closer to paganism—also appeases the divine anger.

In fact, the *hieros gamos* itself is an archetype of the different relationships between the Mesopotamian gods and the biblical God, respectively, with the humans who worship them. In the case of the Babylonians, it is the act of sexual union that seems to be the decisive element (as far as we know of what actually happened). Whatever the nature of this marriage, it has a pronounced Dionysian quality about it. The marriage in Israel celebrates the interpersonal and psychological rather than the biological. God loves Israel, gives her wedding gifts, takes a sweet honeymoon with her in the desert, and brings His bride into a new apartment (the Land of Israel). It is the affection and intimacy *(agape)* of the marriage that are celebrated, not the *eros* (desire) of physical union. In Babylonia, intimacy is not that of love but of passion; it is not dialogue but copulation. Israel's God is less close to man physically but closer emotionally. In Babylonia the god may at times be close physically but never emotionally.

Four

THE GODS AND THE LAW

In order to define the relationships among the gods, the law, and the worshipper in both the Israelite and in the neighboring cultures, one must first clarify the nature or character of the gods themselves and of the law in each case. The following rough comparative scheme can serve as our point of departure.

THE GODS IN MESOPOTAMIA

The Mesopotamian divinities have two main distinguishing characteristics. First, they are not omnipotent or independent, but rather subject to what Yehezkel Kaufmann calls the "meta-divine sphere." They die and are born.[1] They are in need of magical aids in their battles with each other.[2] They must eat or their power is weakened.[3] Eternal and preexistent cosmic laws (*me's*) and tablets of destiny (*ṭuppi-šīmāti*) are not the creation of the gods but forces to which the gods must bend.[4]

Second, the Mesopotamian gods are, in general, indifferent to the human situation. They do not, as a rule, inform men of their will. Their relationship to mankind is like that of a diner to his waiter: other than the service requested, no other connection is expected. Consequently, man feels alone in the world, without direction or instruction. If the gods do not reveal their will to man, man, in his anguish, must find a way to the gods, and if not to their will, at least to their moods. The method used to fathom the mood of the divine spirits is called omenology. The divine moods are thought to be reflected in the stars, in unusual natural phenomena such as earthquakes, and in the viscera of sacrificial animals.

There is reason to believe that the subservience of the gods to fate, nature, and the metadivine sphere and their indifference to the human situation are closely related: one who is completely given over to the satisfaction of his physical needs is not ready for interpersonality.

THE GODS IN GREECE

At the risk of oversimplification, it may be said that there is something narcissistic about much of Greek culture. One of the early ideals of the Greeks was agonistic (from *agon:* "struggle, race"). The highest achievement was to win the contest, whether intellectual, moral, or physical. Thus, one needed the other, less as a Thou, in which one's I found its fulfillment than as a sparring partner against whom one measured one's excellence. Even when the ideal was dialogical, as in the Socratic tradition, the Thou of the philosopher was his male student rather than his wife.

Although one must judge the Greeks on their own terms, one can hardly erase from one's mind the modern theory linking homosexuality and narcissism. The Greek contemplative ideal, however, expresses this inwardness even more clearly. What it strives for is perfection, an essentially static, self-contained condition beyond which nothing more is needed or demanded. In fact, perfection is beyond all need, demand, will, emotion, or individuation of self and non-self. It is the perfect contemplating its own perfection, a state of transcendent non-involvement in the imperfect other.

GOD IN ISRAEL

Paradoxically, the God of Israel, who transcends physical nature (like the Greek prime mover), is nevertheless interested in the world, not for the physical satisfaction of need, like the Meso-potamian gods, but for the spiritual "satisfaction" that only the world of men, with its moral potential, can provide. Speaking poetically, the world of men is both the stage on which the cre-ative plan and play of YHWH is realized and the psychic coun-terpart of the divine "I." Israel is both kinsman of God and partner in the work of creation. The two roles are organically re-lated: only one adopted by YHWH can be entrusted with His plan. The Torah is therefore to be seen in four ways: as (1) the plan entrusted into Israel's hands for realization, (2) the con-tract in which Israel accepts this charge, (3) the history of God's love for His kinsmen, and (4) the contract formalizing this relationship.

Law, in the biblical pattern of culture, is thus a reflection of God's "urge" to create and His "need" for kinsmen. Terms like *urge* and *need,* although used metaphorically, do indicate that God in His biblical manifestation is not contemplatively self-sufficient; however, the need and urge are not physical but spiritual, moral, and transcendent. God desires to realize the Torah, His plan for a moral world, through the instrumentality of the people He loves.

LAW AND RITUAL IN MESOPOTAMIA
AND IN ISRAEL

In Mesopotamia, as we have seen, the ultimate concern of the gods is the food provided by the temple cult.[5] Gods step out of their indifference to complain about the cessation of the temple cult.[6] While the relationship between the gods and the cult is clear, their relationship to justice is ambiguous. First of all, compared with the absolute importance of the cult in the life and existence of the gods, justice on earth is only their penultimate concern, if that. Though they can live with human corruption—as much as they might dislike it—they cannot function at all without the cult.

Furthermore, there are indications that the prevailing norms of justice are not so much a matter of the gods' own will as one of preexisting cosmic principles, inherent laws of the universe that some of the gods administer. J. J. Finkelstein would add another observation: since no god really reigns supreme in the Mesopotamian pantheon, the promulgation of a consistent divine system of law and order is a virtual impossibility.[7] Finally, one must also consider the fact that in spite of all the statements concerning the justice of the gods, humans clearly do not understand how it operates: "What is good in one's sight is evil for a god. What is bad in one's mind is good for his god. Who can understand the counsel of the gods in the midst of heaven?"[8] The gods, being divine, also seem to have the right to be inconsistent. However, whether or not justice is the ultimate concern of divine society, it is the very foundation of human society as conceived by the Mesopotamians. The omnipresent legal tablet is a clear indicator of this Mesopotamian concern for justice.

In Israel, on the other hand, law is the basic concern of the divinity: it is His plan, His play, His "fulfillment." Ritual, although important, is a penultimate concern. God does not castigate the people for lack of sacrifice but for lack of justice. Furthermore, to paraphrase Kaufmann, sacrifice is not needed by God but is given to man as a gift, a way for him to enjoy a modicum of divine intimacy. To overstate the case: in Mesopotamia, ritual is a divine need, law a human one. In Israel, law is a divine need, ritual a human one.[9]

A NEW SCHEMA: TRANSITIVE AND INTRANSITIVE GODS

The generalizations of the previous section are in need of qualification. What follows is derived partly from Thorkild Jacobsen's insights into the nature of Mesopotamian (Sumerian) religion and partly from random comments by Benno Landsberger, the conceptual framework of Teilhard de Chardin, and the philosophical works of Moshe Maisels.[10]

The great historical cultures (China, India, Israel, etc.) are all symbolic attempts to understand man's inner self, each culture seeing a part of the whole. Man's humanity, the structure of his self, is not immediately understood by man but rather is discovered by progressive self-realizations. Furthermore, when man first emerges from the mud of creation, he probably does not differentiate himself much from the world of nature around him. He has a kinship with the landscape, the animals, and the plants. Thus, in the earliest layer of Mesopotamian religion, the gods, always projections of man's sense of himself, are not full-blown personalities but merely symbols of natural forces: the life-giving qualities of milk and the date, the numinous powers of thunder and fire. The gods are not conceived anthropomorphically, as men, but totemistically as the storm cloud, the raven, the *Imdugud* bird, and so forth. Jacobsen calls such nature gods "intransitive."[11]

In the course of time, as man's self-image matures, he comes to see both himself and the gods not merely as impersonal powers but as beings with a will to action and realization, as personalities. Originally intransitive nature gods, portrayed by totemistic symbols, develop more human qualities. In even later times, an interesting conflict emerges. At first, an active, anthropomorphic god will often be accompanied by his older, intransitive manifestation, his preanthropomorphic symbol. However, at a much later date, when the anthropomorphic tendency gains the upper hand, the old cult symbol, the original manifestation of the god, is now juxtaposed against the anthropomorphic manifestation as its enemy! The "human" god fights for its humanity by trampling on the remains of its natural afterbirth. Thus, in the *Enuma Elish*, Ea/Enki, whose original manifestation was *apsû*, "the deep," actually kills *apsû*, one of the helpers of Tiamat!

Mesopotamian religion attempts to liberate the Divine from its natural intransivity, its subservience to the metadivine, and strives toward the greater transitivity of an I-Thou relationship between the Divine and the world. But even its efforts in the latter direction are sporadic and incomplete: the religion as a whole is never able to free itself from its natural afterbirth. The one Near Eastern society that is able to reject intransitivity, with its subservience to nature, and to structure its inner life on the full transitivity of the Divine is Israel. Its God completely transcends nature, *me* (cosmic norms of justice), *ṭuppi-šīmāti* (tablets of destiny), and so on, and is free to express Himself in perfectly transitive, outgoing "human" fashion. To be sure, the biblical insight arises in a cultural environment that is saturated with transitive (if not transcendent) elements.[12]

KING AND PEOPLE AS OBJECTS OF INTEREST

Transitivity expresses itself in love and will: love as a need for personal fulfillment in relation to another self, and will as an urge to realize a plan. If the Mesopotamian gods are never as transitive as the God of Israel, nevertheless, they do have plans, and they do love some humans, not whole nations, as in Israel, but isolated individuals, the kings. For it is the king, not the people, who is the object of divine election and into whose hands is entrusted the plan for a just society.

The Mesopotamian king has two roles: as the *lugal* (ruler) selected by the *puḫrum* (heavenly assembly) and as the *en* (priest) selected by the god. The *en* is the god's partner in sacred marriage. The goddess of the city loves her king, not as administrator but as spouse. The union of god and king is not merely mechanical and magical but personal and emotional as well. Love poems, comparable to the Song of Songs, are composed for the occasion. Furthermore, there is some indication that the divine-royal marriage formulae were not too different from those used in human marriages. For example, when Inanna (the Semitic Ishtar), the goddess of Uruk, tries to seduce Gilgamesh into marriage, she promises him bridal gifts and says: "I am the wife and you are the husband." That this is probably the same formula used in human marriages is reflected in Hosea 2 and in the Elephantine papyri.

The will/plan of the transitive gods also expresses itself in a relationship to the king as *lugal,* rather than to the people. Even though the gods do not create the cosmic norms of justice *(me)* but are only entrusted with them, they do have an independent urge to see them realized in the world. This divine plan for social justice is reflected quite clearly in the prologues to the Old Babylonian codes, those of Lipit-Ishtar and Hammurabi. The gods select these two kings, not merely to restore temples and unify the land, but also and mainly, to secure social justice, to see that the rich did not afflict the poor. Thus the gods are the source of the plan and of the will to realize it, while the people are merely a passive stage upon which the plan for social justice *(kittum u mēšarum)* is to be realized,[13] as we see in the following chart:

me	God	King	People
preexisting source of law	will to realization	agent of realization	object/stage; promulgator of law

By contrast, in Israel, the transitivity of the Divine is enlarged to the breaking point: God is no longer subservient to preexisting *me,* whether cosmic or legal. It is He who preexists; therefore, He is the source of the law. However, His is also its will to realization. In these two roles, He combines the functions of Mesopotamian *me* and the Mesopotamian gods. However, like the Mesopotamian king, He is also the promulgator of the laws. Furthermore, His absolute transcendence has two corollaries: (1) since He has no natural needs, His only and total concern is now with justice and law; and (2) the object of His transitivity is enlarged. That is, He expresses His love, not by electing one man (the king) to translate His plan into reality, but by electing a whole people (Israel) for this task. Thus, in terms of these functions, the people of Israel, the object of God's love and the executor of His plan for social justice, is the equivalent of the Mesopotamian king. At the same time, the people are also the stage on which the drama is to be played out. Thus, the following schema emerges:

God	People
source of law (= *me*)	object of love (= king)
will to realization (= gods)	agent of realization (= king)
promulgator (= king)	stage on which plan is realized (= people)

The observation that the people of Israel in its collectivity has the dignity of a Mesopotamian king fits nicely with an insight shared with me many years ago by Finkelstein: only the sin of the king really counts in Mesopotamia; the sins of laymen are a matter of divine indifference.[14] You can only really be angry with someone you care about. Consequently, since all Israelites are functionally in the position of the Mesopotamian king—the objects of divine interest—even the sins of individuals are enough to stir the divine wrath. In stating that all Jews were "like sons of kings," the Rabbis were not overstating the case.

THE COLLECTIVITY

In Israel, the idea of peoplehood also takes on new meaning. The West Semites (Arabs, Arameans, proto-Israelites, the non-sedentary population of Old Babylonian Mari) all seem to have preserved a tribal society that had long disappeared in southern Mesopotamia. West Semitic society was based on the blood affinities of family and clan, while the urban society of southern Mesopotamia was based on political association within a city and the concomitant urban social stratification into *awīlu* (aristo-crat), *muškēnu* (commoner), and *wardu* (slave). There is no doubt that the ancestors of Israel were closer to the West Semitic social order than to the southern Mesopotamian one: the patriarchal records bear at least superficial witness to a tribal system in which racial identity—and racial purity—are of great importance.

But despite these reflexes of a tribal mentality, there is lit-tle doubt in the minds of most scholars that the historical Israel was not simply the natural offspring of an original father, Abra-ham, or even of the twelve sons of Jacob. All now assume that almost every racial and ethnic element in the Near East of the second millennium—Canaanite, Habiru, Egyptian, West Semitic, Mesopotamian, proto-Aramean—was incorporated into the new Israelite people.[15] This heterogeneous racial mass was molded into a "people," not by a natural process of reproduc-tion, but by the catalyst of the new religious movement. Or, to revert to the terminology used above, the disparate ethnic ele-ments out of which Israel was formed were fused together into a new political-religious organism by virtue of being selected as the object of divine interest to be the agents of the divine plan. Such an organization is neither a tribal people *('am)*, like the West Semites, nor a political nation *(goy, in E. A. Speiser's ter-minology), like the Mesopotamians.[16] Rather, it is the model of a new form of social organization: the "church," a familylike or-ganization, all of whose members, regardless of their biological ancestry, consider one another as brothers descended from the "founding fathers" and that all people may join by accepting certain basic theological tenets or, in the case of ancient religions, laws.[17]

FAMILY AND NATION: TWO VERSIONS OF NATIONAL FORMATION

Two entirely different pictures of Israel's early history emerge from the biblical account. According to the Priestly version, Israel was not yet God's kinfolk in the patriarchal period and therefore did not know God's secret personal name. The divine *b'rit* (covenant) with Abram is one sided: YHWH becomes his god and protector, but Abram and his relatives do not yet become God's people. Sinai thus becomes the most significant incident in the life of the religious community, for it is there that Israel's religious and ethnic status is radically changed. There the Israelites are adopted by God, becoming His kinsmen and thus enjoying the intimate privilege of knowing His personal name, withheld even from the greats of antiquity, who had not yet reached this blessed status.

In this account, although the patriarchs set the scene, it is Moses who appears as the great religious innovator and the creator of an *ethnos*, a people, out of the preexisting ethnic elements whose origins are rooted in the Near East of the second millennium. This is essentially the viewpoint of Yehezkel Kaufmann, who, although not denying the authentic local color of the patriarchal stories or the historicity of the patriarchs, does not consider them monotheists and thus denies their creative function in the history of biblical religion. Moses thus becomes the focus of attention; it is his religious genius that intuits the new faith and in its fire forges the new people, who are to bear the new religion and shape its destiny.

The picture that emerges from JE is entirely different.* The experience of Sinai is, in this view, not a radical religious break in the traditions of Israel. It does not bring with it the revelation of a new god whom the patriarchs did not know, nor does it change the familial status of Israel in relation to the God it knew of old, since Israel was already the kinsman of YHWH in the time of Abraham. In fact, without this understanding, the divine promise to Abram is quite meaningless. God promises to convert Abram, who is already His *'am* (kinsman), into a *goy (polis)*. In the JE version of Exodus, God redeems *(padah)* His *'am:* they are already His people. At Sinai, however, He fulfills His promise to convert this family into a *goy qadosh,* a political organization set apart in might from the rest of the *goyim* of the world. As most of the commentators, old and new, have noted, *qadosh* here means taboo, sacrosanct, set apart—holy, not in the moral sense, but in the sense that it cannot be used for ordinary purposes. The term conveys the promise of YHWH to set Israel up as a powerful state, not His demand that they be, in the religious sense, a holy people (this demand is found only in P).

This picture of Sinai as religiously, though not politically, continuous with the earlier patriarchal narrative in JE thus stresses Abraham's creative role in setting the biblical process in motion—the realization that his *'am* (which simply exists and is not created) is the carrier of a new religious movement derived from, but opposed to, the preexisting religious traditions of both Mesopotamia and Egypt. Moses, then, is not the religious

---

* Modern Bible source criticism divides the Torah into four sources indicated by one-letter abbreviations J, E, P, and D; J = Jahwistic source, E = Elohist source, P = Priestly source, and D = Deuteronomic source. The siglum JE indicates the composite text composed of J and E.

innovator, but the political genius who is able to translate the dream of the *'am* into the structured political reality of a nation bound by a covenant and its curses, by a law and its coercive power. According to this view, the ethnic unit Israel did not have to be created; it was the natural genetic datum, the raw material at hand, identical with the family of Abram, out of which the later *goy* was to be forged. Peoplehood was a fact of nature; nationhood was a creative act.

According to the Priestly view, however, nothing is a fact of nature; even the supposedly natural body, the *'am*, comes into being not by the organic process of birth, but by the artificial means of divine adoption. All other peoples are born; Israel is created. The process of converting natural entities into created ones is not limited to peoples; the holiness of Jerusalem, for example, is not natural but an act of divine selection—of accident, not of essence. Which of these antithetical points of view reflects the actual course of events is hard to tell.

Based on these two different theological viewpoints, one could take either of two perspectives in dating the two different strands. Some have argued that the apolitical quality of P reflects the apolitical conditions of the exilic period, where the church, not the state, was the dominant institution of national life. JE's political vision, according to this view, mirrors a more ancient idea of a state and nation, an idea that may have been cultivated by the prestate *'am* in its original condition. The idea that this vision of the nation antedates its settlement in Palestine should be viewed in light of Kaufmann's theory that the unreal borders attributed by the Bible to the Promised Land represent a similar preconquest vision, rather than, as most scholars understand it, a prophecy after the fact. In any case, both are visions to be fulfilled, not fulfillments piously projected into the past.

THE COVENANT IN PROPHETIC TEXTS

It seems to me, however, that another approach to this question is more logical. As Kaufmann has pointed out, the period of the exile is anything but apolitical. The ecclesia of this time is a political necessity imposed on the people from without by historical forces not under their control. It is not the will of the people; on the contrary, their violently political eschatology is a clear indication of their antiecclesiastical tendencies. Rather, we must consider the apolitical vision of P as an authentic reflection of the prestate mentality of a people *('am)* living under divine kingship, a mentality reflected vividly in the books of Joshua and Judges, but one that broke down under the impact of Philistine political power.

JE's political emphasis is thus later than the apolitical P and reflects the political expansionism of the early monarchy (this is when JE is commonly dated anyway), when the initial religious antagonism toward "secular" kingship has been overcome. By this time, Davidic rule has been so thoroughly integrated into the national consciousness that it is considered to represent a new divine covenant and dispensation to Israel. The early history is then reinterpreted in the light of this golden era of Israelite statehood. In no other period, either earlier or later, could the political dream have been identified with the religious promise of old.

But there are other complexities to be considered in the relationships of the prophetic books to the covenant of the *'am,* which emerge from 2 Samuel, from Deuteronomy, and especially from Jeremiah. In the oracle of Nathan, in 2 Samuel 7, God speaks repeatedly of Israel as His *'am,* and adopts the king ("I will be his father, and he will be My son") as He adopted Israel. In his prayer of thanksgiving for this oracle, David mentions the liberation from Egypt, including both political and spiritual elements:

> And who is like Your *'am*, like Israel, a unique nation *(goy)* in the world, whom God went and redeemed for Himself as a people, ... Your people, whom You redeemed for Yourself from Egypt...? You established Your people Israel for Yourself as a people forever, and You, O YHWH, became their God. (2 Sam. 7:23–24)

From this passage it is clear that the idea that Israel became God's *'am* at Sinai is very old, no matter what one says about the antiquity of P.

Another thing is clear: the *'am* idea does not appear here in the purity of P; rather, it is combined with the *goy* idea of JE. These two ideas are fused together by the author of David's psalm (we do not consider this passage reworked by the Deuteronomic editor) and become the normative theology of Deuteronomy, which also merges the two ideas in its own, not-always-clear fashion. On the basis of this passage from Samuel, we would suggest that the *'am/goy* stratum in D also dates from about the time of David. There is more of the *goy* theology than the *'am* theology, which would point to the time of the Davidic monarchy; kingship is at least a possibility although not an altogether concrete reality. The similarity between this Deuteronomic stance and the kinship passage in Samuel is most striking. D as a religious tract does not omit the more spiritual *'am* theology and is almost identical in tenor with David's prayer.

The subsequent adaptation of the two theologies by the literary prophets is of great interest. Some of these prophets (Amos, Micah) merely echo eschatologically the promise of political might inherent in the theology of the *goy*. Others, like Hosea, Jeremiah, and Second Isaiah, activate the religiously more evocative theme inherent in the theology of the *'am*. The promise of the Sinaitic covenant is of familial intimacy with the Divine, not political supremacy. Lack of faith is not to be punished so much by political subjugation as by radical estrangement from the family of YHWH. This estrangement is described dramatically as a temporary annulment of the marriage at Sinai; and it is this psychological moment that is the decisive punishment, not the external pain of death, famine, or exile. Both the divine love and the divine hatred are described in more radical terms than they are in the political narrative of JE.

In JE, Israel as God's people is a biological given; the annulment of this natural relationship is never even considered. Obedience brings political success, while faithlessness brings political calamity. The whole discussion has an outward, objective quality to it. It does not partake of the sweetness and intimacy of a newly formed family relationship, so cherished just because it is created and not to be taken for granted. But such created, "artificial" family ties are of a delicate, tenuous nature. Any lack of love on the part of the adoptee can destroy them; coolness, anger, and a subsequent repudiation may follow. It is this psychological polarity of intimacy and anger that typifies and inspirits the Priestly narrative. And it is this theology that later inspires the subjective pleadings of prophets like Hosea, Jeremiah, and Second Isaiah. Though the imagery of the prophets is much more daring and dramatic than that of the rather Apollonian Priestly texts, they are carrying on in the same theological tradition.

Most significantly it is the Priestly narrative, famed for its hieratical dryness, and not the colorful and exuberant JE source, that places great emphasis on the inner, the psychological, and the emotional. This is a warning to those who overlook the warmth and the depth of the inner life often present in ritualistic religion. It was from this source that Jeremiah drew part of his inspiration for the oracle of the New Covenant. This may sound strange and even absurd to many modern scholars who, while realizing the great antiquity of much material in P, still insist on considering the "general framework" as postexilic. Following Kaufmann, however, we see it as quite natural for Jeremiah to have been influenced not only by D but also by other ancient priestly material found in proto-P. In fact, Kaufmann has already collected several cogent examples of such borrowing. The dependence of the New Covenant oracle in Jeremiah 31 on the promises of love and the curses of rejection in Leviticus 26 is just one more example of the same process, in which the *'am* theology of P appears in the passion of the literary prophets.

PART II

THE DIVINE PERSON

Six

BIBLICAL ANTHROPOMORPHISM

There is a root tension in the nature of YHWH, the God of Israel. On the one hand, He is utterly other than the stuff of the world or its laws. He is the principle of absolute nondependence. Neither magic nor fate controls Him. Destiny is not prior to Him. He is not born, and He does not die. And yet, at the same time, this being of total nondependence is portrayed in the Bible as having qualities that can only be described as human.[1]

This problem of biblical anthropomorphism has still to find a critical yet sympathetic treatment. Accepted literally and vulgarized by the simple minded, the biblical portrayal of God has been laughed at by the pagans as overrational and lacking vitality or harmony with the cosmic processes. Sophisticated mystics have rejected it as unspiritual and too involved with the world. Classical philosophers would probably have dismissed the all-too-human God of the Hebrew Bible as just another "barbaric" myth. Monotheistic theologians—Jewish and Muslim— are also in an uncomfortable position, because they feel the truth of God's personhood, yet realize that the absolute cannot be human in any real sense. They have neither the radical skepticism of philosophy nor the fire of myth. What they are left with is a person who is not much of a personality.[2]

The historically and phenomenologically sophisticated exegete of today may take care not to caricature the anthropomorphism of YHWH in the writings of ancient Israel, but philosophically he cannot have much sympathy for it. If God's absoluteness means His utter nonidentification with the world and His freedom from the coercion of eternal law or fate, then the attribution to Him of an unfulfilled will or desire—a desire that can only be satisfied by an independent human agent and that, being unfulfilled, causes Him dismay and regret—limits God's autonomy, the hallmark of His divinity. Although not subservient to preexisting nature, as in paganism, He is, somehow, according to the biblical myth, subject to the demands of His personality and to the caprice of the humans He created.

For many philosophically inclined readers, this mythical characterization of YHWH can be seen as a mere epiphenomenon, an accident of birth in which a metaphysical idea of absolute transcendence manifests itself in certain historical situations in a relatively primitive way. Perhaps such anthropomorphism is just a matter of style, not of content, an accident of history rather than the essence of biblical religion. The personalism of biblical faith remains an attenuated form of paganism because it sets limits to God's autonomy, and the monotheistic revolution is only complete when the principle of autonomy has shed completely the husk of mythical personalism.[3]

However, I suggest that God's transcendence and personalism are *complementary* rather than *contradictory:* only a being in control of nature (including His own nature) can act with the freedom needed to involve Himself in the human world. The tension between the concept of transcendence, which insists the Deity is not to be identified with the *physis* of the world, and radical personalism, which insists the Deity is anthropomorphically involved in the world, is the very source of the creative dynamism of biblical monotheism.[4]

In contrast, there is a whole group of post-Buberian scholars who have tried to grapple with the problem of biblical anthropomorphism by, in a sense, embracing it.[5] The anthropomorphic imagery, they say, reflects an underlying truth: that the God of Israel is *sublime* but not *abstract*. Unfortunately, their efforts have not been successful. Some of them fail to account, etiologically or phenomenologically, for the polarity of divine transcendence and divine interest in the world. This is a failure of omission: they do not take either this polarity or the process of God's transcendence, His "growing up," seriously.

The problem with these approaches is that character, including divine character, can only be understood through the categories of art and psychology.[6] God should be studied with the same literary sensitivity that Erich Auerbach, in *Mimesis,* applies to David and Abraham.[7] We need not abandon, only temporarily suspend, considerations of faith and philosophy in order to savor the personality before us, fictitious or not. We must consider not only YHWH's love but also His anger and the human capacity to mollify it. We must realize that in their mythical relation to God, humans are not merely the passive recipients of the Divine Monarch's grace, as depicted in the catechism of God-in-history, but also free agents summoned to satisfy some strange need in the Divine. They are called upon to realize God's law, not merely to be touched by His salvation.[8]

Even Edmond Cherbonnier, who considers that YHWH is not all-knowing or all-seeing, and Abraham Joshua Heschel, who reckons with certain aspects of the divine anger, do not face head-on the mythical representation of the divine ego in its fullness.[9] The mode is still theological rather than literary. But to be understood properly, the divine need, which Yehezkel Kaufmann has to reject as epiphenomenal and Heschel can accept only as something profound and transcendent, must be seen, at least at first glance, as a projection of simple human need—not physical, as divine need is in Mesopotamian paganism, but psychological.

That is the problem with another school of biblical research, certainly not philosophical in character, that would at first seem likely to be more sympathetic to the use of anthropomorphism. Rather than focusing on divine transcendence as the unique feature of biblical religion, this school centers its attention on the fact that YHWH—not caught up in the cyclical rhythm of nature like the gods of Mesopotamia—is a god who reveals Himself in the course of human history in acts of saving grace, celebrated in the cultic litanies of Israel.[10] The key to this understanding of God is *Heilsgeschichte,* the idea that God works in history through human agency. While this approach is certainly correct in stressing His active and concerned relationship with humanity, it rarely spells out what this historical emphasis implies about God as a person rather than a mere idea. Simply put, why does God express Himself in time by acts of saving grace? What does this tell us about His character? The idea of history seems more important here than the quality of personality. One would also like to know if there is any relationship between the historical-temporal mode of God's self-expression and His freedom from nature. But this question, being seen perhaps as too psychological, is rarely raised.

Those who do try to spell out some of the personal implications of the *Heilsgeschichte* myth do so in terms of an (implicit) *eros-agape* model.[11] In philosophical paganism, humans are drawn to the gods by *eros* (desire) and devote their efforts to satisfying their needs. In monotheism—including that of the Hebrew Bible—God is drawn to humans, and His grace is an expression of *agape,* freely bestowed, for they can give Him nothing (or at least nothing comparable) in return. This reversal of pagan spirituality, from down-up to up-down, so pronounced in Christianity, is first adumbrated in the covenantal relationship set forth in the Hebrew Bible, where YHWH (much in the fashion of an ancient Near Eastern monarch) saves Israel from Egypt and in an act of free will allies Himself with Israel for all time.[12] God is the initiator of the process, the source of grace; Israel is the passive recipient. Thus, the personal implications of *Heilsgeschichte* are clearly spelled out: God is a god of *agape,* and it is this selfless love that expresses itself in history.[13]

While there is indeed an element of *agape* in covenantal theology, it is not the whole story. By overstressing this element, most students of the Bible tend to flatten God's personalism and play down His drama in favor of a more abstract concept of the Deity. By allowing God to be outgoing and transitive only in the condescending manner of a king, by denying Him the "humanity" of somehow needing human action for His own fulfillment, they actually deprive the myth of its radical character. In fact, while the God of *agape* is human in His concern for mankind, He is not human in His independence. The law-giving God, on the other hand, is most human—too human—in His desire for the realization of the law, His frustration and anger over its nonfulfillment, and His willingness to allow mortals to control His anger so as to avoid destroying the world.[14]

A reading of the ancient Near Eastern suzerainty treaties in light of the *agape* model gives us the condescending personalism of a king who, needing nothing, bestows favor on an inferior. There is no doubt that this tonality is heard in many passages of the Hebrew Bible. God is terrible in His majesty yet has saved Israel in His grace. But other notes are heard too, for example, in connection with the so-called monarchical selection of Israel in the desert. According to one source, the reason that God hardened Pharaoh's heart was to spread His fame in the world (e.g., Exod. 7:3–5). In a sense, YHWH was a young God without any reputation. He was starting His career, and this extraordinary exercise of His power was an effective way of gaining a reputation—which He soon did. This is a God with human needs, and the myth describes their satisfaction. Just as He is concerned about making a name for Himself, so is He concerned about losing it. "What will the Egyptians say?" asks

Moses. And why will God redeem Israel in the end of days? To clear His name! This is hardly the God of utter transcendence.

God saves Israel, then, not simply as a matter of condescension to the needy, but as a means of securing His own reputation. But fame is not enough; He also wants a family. So He goes to the slave market of antiquity, manumits a group of slaves (Israel), adopts them as His kin, and gives them a paternity, on condition that they do His bidding.[15] YHWH the savior may be a transcendent, condescending monarch, but His commandment to a people to carry out His laws springs from a creative urge to see an unrealized plan fulfilled in the world. It was for this reason that the divine plan is delegated to a people, for this reason that God is angry over its nonfulfillment, and for this reason that God allows His anger to be cooled by mortals in such a human way.[16] It is clear, then, that we are dealing with a most human God.

Seven

THE LIVING MACHINE

The *merkabah*, the mystic chariot whose description begins the book of Ezekiel, is a living machine, studded with eyes. As a machine it is not alive but, paradoxically, made up of living creatures. One face is that of an eagle, another that of a lion, a third that of a bull. The last is the face of a man. The *merkabah*'s interior is a fiery furnace, probably the combustion chamber where the explosive energy is generated whereby this multicreatured machine is empowered and moved. On top of this fiery furnace is a cool slab of lapis lazuli upon which, on a throne of the same stone, sits the man-God YHWH, wearing an upper garment closely fitted to His body and a plumed skirt of fire.

Historically speaking, we have here a fusion of several well-known elements. It has been suggested that the inanimate parts of this chariot are patterned after the laving utensils used in the desert tabernacle and in Solomon's temple. The idea that God sits on a throne is mentioned in Isaiah 6 and in many psalms. That His throne-dais is a slab of lapis lazuli is known from Exodus 24, in which Moses and the elders sit and eat in the presence of God, whose throne-dais is said to be "as pure as the very heavens above." That God rides forth on a chariot is also well established from many biblical passages. What we have here is the fusion of the God-sitting-on-His-throne image with that of God-riding-His-chariot. Usually, when God moves, no mention is made of a throne. Here, God sits on His throne when He travels forth to visit His people.

Ezekiel's Mesopotamian background may have had some influence on the prophet's imagination, since pictures of Mesopotamian gods portray them sitting on their thrones, which are then placed on chariots, which in turn are loaded onto boats, when these gods come from the various cities of Mesopotamia to visit the head of the pantheon on solemn occasions. It is inconceivable that Ezekiel was not familiar with the imagery of such processions.

Ezekiel's innovation is not merely in combining throne with chariot imagery, but also—and especially—in stressing that the structure of the chariot is made up of living beings. Even though it is a chariot with wheels, these wheels have living eyes within them. So, even in its inanimacy, the *merkabah* is animated by the *ruah*(spirit). The machinery symbolizes the omnipresence of YHWH sitting on His throne, which is moved by a chariot composed of the noblest beasts (the lion and the bull), the noblest of birds (the eagle), and the noblest of creatures (man). It is most fitting that God's chariot be drawn by representatives of the noblest of living creatures. They are not divine but do play a creative role as members of God's entourage. This bespeaks a great love for the natural and the living, as well as an almost ecumenical spirit. The whole complex symbolizes the omnipresent concern of the deity.

The eyes, especially, symbolize keen interest, whether for good or for evil. The good eye worries about man. Does he have enough food, enough water? Is he in trouble, in need of redemption? Does he need a friend? The other eye is constantly probing the world and man's heart for sins that he may have committed. Has man been just? Has he honored his parents? Has he done righteous deeds? If not, why not and where? This is the eye that punishes. And then, of course, there is the "evil eye," about which we won't speak.

Now the good eye, as Deuteronomy (11:12) puts it, watches over Israel from the beginning of the year to the end, seeking only Israel's good. In Zechariah 4:10, we find the candelabrum, the seven branches of which are said to be the eyes of YHWH, which roam the world. It is said of this menorah that its stems are filled with living eyes, which can only mean that the machinelike candelabrum, too, is a living organism. If the spouts of the menorah are God's eyes, then by implication the menorah has to be—or at least symbolize—none other than God Himself. In some ways, then, there is a structural parallel between the menorah—living and filled with eyes—and the *merkabah* of Ezekiel.

In rabbinic literature it is said that God's eyes are like those of the deer, which sleeps with one eye opened and the other closed.[1] It is awake and alert, even when it is asleep. God, were He to sleep (which He doesn't), would, so to speak, do so with one eye open, out of His providential concern for Israel. According to the Zohar, God's eyes are like those of the fish, which has no lids and is always awake, always alert.[2]

God's not sleeping means that He is always alert to the needs of His people, as it says: "He who guards Israel neither slumbers nor sleeps" (Ps. 121:4). Yet, for poetic reasons, Second Isaiah comes close to attributing a catnap to the Deity when he says: "Upon your walls, O Jerusalem, I have set watchmen, who shall never be silent, by day or by night. O you, YHWH's remembrancers, do not sleep and do not let Him sleep, until He establish Jerusalem and make her renowned on earth" (62:6). So much for those who would attribute an anti-anthropomorphic tendency to Second Isaiah.

It should be noted in passing that the so-called eye of YHWH may be a reflection of a well-known institution found in human royal courts. Kings always had functionaries—today they might be called secretaries or major domos—whose task was to remind the king of his calendar of appointments: when he was to go here and when there, when he was to speak to the chamber of commerce, when he was to dedicate a bridge. According to Isaiah, God's unsleeping eye has only one function, the noblest of all: to remind Him day and night that Jerusalem is to be restored to its former glory. What a marvelous role it enjoys!

Since we are dealing with the theme of divine alertness, of God's metaphorical sleeping and awakening, it may be of interest to note that in the ancient world, it was a common practice, when the sun rose, for the priests of all temples to open their gates and, by the singing of hymns, wake up the deity, reminding him that his temple was in good condition and that its altars were laden with the best foods available, ready for his immediate consumption. This practice is well attested in Egypt, Greece, Mesopotamia, and, surprisingly enough, in the Temple of YHWH in Jerusalem. Here, a group of priests—literally, the awakeners—would sing the hymn "Arise, O YHWH, Don't Sleep." Even though this had been an ancient custom in Jerusalem, John Hyrkanus abolished the practice, as it seemed to smack of paganism and overstep the limits of propriety (*Sotah* 9:10). That this danger was constantly lurking for those who preferred a personal, anthropomorphic god to an abstract philosophical one is clear. It is the creative tension between the abstract and the concrete that underpins any real religion.

Eight

DIVINE ASPIRATIONS:

FOUR ASPECTS OF KINGSHIP

In my original thinking on the personality of the Divine, I followed a kind of psychogenesis, a child development theory observing the stages laid down by Thorkild Jacobsen.[1] The first phase is that of the intransitive god, which emphasizes the potency in nature. God may be described as an udder, a tree, a date. This is followed by what I like to call the Jolly Green Giant stage, where the ear of corn suddenly sprouts a face. The personality is emerging but is still caught up in the husk. The third phase is a fully transitive one, where the God manifests both a will and plan. The husk is stripped of its natural origins to become a fully articulated person. The husk becomes the enemy He fights against. But this stage remains limited, for the personality is nothing more than that of a teenager fighting with his origins, against parental authority.

The fourth phase is what we recognize as biblical religion. Natural limitations have been fully transcended, leading not to abstraction but to greater humanization.[2] The being is totally free to express itself in an interpersonal manner. Superiority over nature is a precondition of his interpersonal relations; that is, the

Creator of nature is now in a position to become a loving God or loving person.

In what follows, we will explore four aspects, or stages, of this interpersonal drama: (1) God, as a young independent deity, trying to establish His reputation and power in humanity and elect a particular group of people as His personal following; (2) God showing His ability and desire to provide all the necessities to this newly elected people; (3) God trying to establish a trusting relationship from His elected by submitting Himself to impious rational questioning; and (4) God acting as a fully established and confident king whose purpose is to show benevolence and mercy to His people.

I. GOD THE YOUNG HERO

Seen mythically, God, as He appears in Exodus, is like a young hero at the beginning of his career. His desire is to get Himself a reputation and to acquire a family. Like many childless couples in antiquity, He went to the slave market called Egypt, manumitted a slave (Israel), adopted him ("I shall be your God and you shall be my people") on condition that the son—who was now on a first-name basis ("YHWH," no longer *El Shaddai* [Powerful God]) with the adoptive father, being a member of the family—serve him loyally all his life. As a reward for this loyal service, the son/manumitted slave would receive a rich patrimony—in their case, the land of Israel.

During the course of this drama of liberation and adoption, especially during the cat-and-mouse game of God's "hardening the Pharaoh's heart," YHWH makes for Himself a great name. In fact, it was just for this purpose—namely, to spread the reputation of God's power—that the whole drama was set up and staged: "Nevertheless I have spared you for this purpose: in order to show you My power, and in order that My fame shall resound throughout the world" (Exod. 9:16).[3]

In this somewhat mythical retelling of the story, our major metaphor has been that of slave becoming son, yet the actual use of the word *son* in the Exodus narrative is extremely rare. The Israelites are called *benei Yisrael*, "sons of Israel," but not "My sons." There is, however, one notable exception. In Exodus 4:22–23, we read: "Then you shall say to Pharaoh, 'Thus says YHWH: Israel is My firstborn son. I have said to you, *shlaḥ 'et bni ve-ya'avdeni* [Let My son go, that he may worship Me].'" The phrase *shlaḥ 'et bni ve-ya'avdeni* is paralleled by Exodus 5:1: *shlaḥ 'et 'ammi ve-yaḥogu li bamidbar* [Let My people go that they may celebrate a festival for Me in the wilderness].

In Deuteronomy 26:17–19, we find that the declaration "I will be your God and you shall be my people" is reformulated in the direction of a greater mutuality: Israel is no longer a passive actor in the drama of adoption/marriage. She no longer has declarations simply directed to her, but makes her own declaration, an expression of her own free will: "You have affirmed … that YHWH is your God.... And YHWH has affirmed this day that you are … His treasured people … and that He will set you, in *shem, tehillah,* and *tif'eret* [fame, renown, and glory], high above all the nations that He had made." From this context, it is clear that these three qualities of *shem, tehillah,* and *tif'eret* are Israel's reward for having elected YHWH and having served Him faithfully. Israel will be on top of the nations and a sacrosanct people to YHWH—untouchable, protected.

In Jeremiah 13 this idiomatic cluster of *shem, tehillah,* and *tif'eret* is reshaped and recycled in an illuminating manner. Jeremiah is commanded to buy a linen tunic and wear it but not to clean it with water. The prophet does what he is told. YHWH appears to him a second time. This time he is commanded to take the garment, go to a neighboring stream, and bury it in a crack in a rock, where it disintegrates until "it is good for nothing." God explains to the prophet the significance of the act: the tunic is sinful Israel. "So just as a tunic has a pressing body, so I have hugged Israel close to me for *shem, tehillah,* and *tif'eret,* but they have not listened" (Jer. 13:11). A man wears a new suit to look good. God "wore Israel" as a suit of clothes that He might "look good."

Clearly in this context the "glory and splendor" are no longer Israel's but are now applied to God, who elected Israel to reflect His glory. But they did not do so and were, therefore, consigned to destruction. What is significant here is that the idiom which was originally used in a context of religious imperialism is now creatively reused to reflect the pathetic God's feeling of His disappointment with a people who did not live up to His expectation.

But the story is not over. The rejection of Israel, symbolized by the disintegrated cloak, is not a permanent condition. In Jeremiah 33, we read about an eschatological forgiveness of sin: "[This act of forgiveness] will be to Me for *shem sasson* [joyful renown], for *tehillah* and *tif'eret* [renown and splendor], for all the nations of the earth who will hear about all the good things I am doing for them" (33:9). Linguistically, Jeremiah adds to the cluster *shem, tehillah,* and *tif'eret* the term *sasson* (joy).

In Isaiah 61:3, we read: "To provide for the mourners in Zion—To give them *pe'er* [a turban] instead of *'efer* [ashes], *shemen sasson* [festive ointment] instead of mourning, *ma'ate tehillah* [a garment of splendor] instead of drooping spirit. They shall be called terebinths of victory, planted by YHWH *lehitpa'er* [for His glory]." Notice that all the elements of Jeremiah 33 are present, the *shemen sasson* being a development of the earlier *shem, tehillah,* and *tif'eret* in the expression *ma'ate tehillah,* and *lehitpa'er.* What is noteworthy about this passage is not merely the skillful reshaping of older elements, but also the echo of the cloak of Jeremiah 13: *pe'er* (a turban) and *ma'ate* (a cloak).[4]

The "name" the young hero God has made for Himself has shifted in this cluster from an imperialistic national fame, to a divine desire that Israel by its deeds might reflect God's glory, to an eschatological act of forgiveness by which God reestablishes His reputation and, in the language of Ezekiel, "clears his desecrated name" (36:23).

II. GOD THE PROVIDER

It is often said, quite well by Heschel, that the Bible is the book of divine concern and involvement.[5] God's involvement manifests itself in His making a covenant with Israel. To some degree, man is a copartner with God in establishing a moral world. However, prior to this two-way involvement—a product of some sophistication—is the God who provides and saves, who almost needs to be needed. He craves situations that demand His sustaining care.

Thus in Psalm 50, it is as if God is looking for an opportunity to save man and elicit his thanks for His saving power: "Just call on me and I will extricate you" (50:15). Similarly in Malachi 3:10, God seems to plead:

> Please, just test me, said YHWH of Hosts.
> I will surely open the floodgates of the sky for you
> and pour down boundless blessings.

God's providence, like everything else in the Bible, is presented not as a theological abstraction but in a series of concrete situations figuratively conceived. God's concern for man begins before birth. God the gynecologist is intimately concerned with all aspects of childbirth. He knows what goes on in the womb of both man and beast.

In answer to Job's questions concerning divine justice, God puts him off by overwhelming him with examples of divine power or, shall we say, concern:

> Do you know which month every pregnant animal is in?
> Do you then feed every animal according to its own
> diet and in its proper time?[6] (cf. Job 38:39–39:4)

69

The noble lion that utters a triumphant roar when he has caught his own breakfast (cf. Amos 3:4) is converted by the Bible into the dependent client of God who supplicates the deity with a roarlike prayer to provide him with his food: "The young lions roar for prey, seeking their food from God" (Ps. 104:21). Human and animal needs are connected with the divine need to provide, in much the same way as the social worker needs human problems for his own self-fulfillment. As the Rabbis have it, God's concern encompasses all reality, from the eggs of the bedbug to the horns of the wild oxen.[7]

Beyond all of the divine concern to provide for all His creatures, however, it is truly amazing how concerned God is about His ability to provide food for His own people. He is especially disturbed by Moses's sarcastic remark: "If all the sheep and cattle of the world were slaughtered and all the fish of the sea gathered up, would this be sufficient for them?" (Num. 11:22). He is equally incensed over the people's question: "Is God really able to set a table in the desert? We have seen that He can hit rocks so that water will gush forth and streams quickly flow, but is He also able to provide bread and can He supply His people with flesh?" (Ps. 78:19–20). The sequel is well known. "He rained *(va-yamṭer)* upon them the manna to eat and He gave them corn of heaven, bread of the powerful angels, mortal men ate.... He rained upon them meat like dust and like the sand of the ocean, He rained upon them winged birds" (Ps. 78:24–27). The verb *himṭir* usually refers to destructive storms of hail and rain. As if to say, "Food you want? Food you'll get!" God gives in this case with a vengeance. One is reminded of the Gilgamesh epic where Ea, in discussing how Gilgamesh should behave during his construction of the ark, tells him: "[When the people ask you what you are doing, just say that my god] is about to rain upon you a rain of *kibāti*," which in Akkadian has two distinct meanings: "wheat" and "blight."[8]

In these passages God appears as the angry provider.

"They have dared to doubt my ability to provide. I'll provide for them until it runs out of their nose." This is hardly the normal attitude of God. In fact, there seem to be passages when God actually begs Israel to test His goodness. God—in the light of His tested (proven) record of providential care for Israel—is naturally hurt that Israel runs after other gods for salvation and physical sustenance (e.g. Ezek. 16 and Hos. 2). God is the divine cornucopia: "I am YHWH your God who liberated you from Egypt. Open wide your mouth and I will fill it with (good)" (Ps. 81:11). I can only take this as an almost pathetic request to try YHWH's bounty: "Test Me and you will see how good I am." The concluding verses seem to confirm this reality: "If My people Israel would only listen to Me and follow My path, then I would defeat your enemies soundly ... and I would feed you with the cream of wheat and would sate you with honey from the rock" (Ps. 81:14–17). *If* only they would try me! You think that the nature gods of the nations can provide an abundance? Just test me and I will outdo them at their own game. For only I am your real provider—*Elohekha*. (See Hosea 12:10 for a similar theme.) One of the major functions of the pagan gods was to provide rain. According to Jeremiah, God can outrain the rainmakers (Hebrew, *magshim*, literally "rainmaker"): "Do the heavens (of themselves) provide rains?" (14:22).

God not only provides food and water on a regular basis or miraculously when it is desperately needed, as was the case in the desert. He also is miraculously able to convert bad food into a marvelously nourishing substance. This is God's role as curer of the curse that some substances have by nature. Thus, in Exodus, when the Israelites came to Marah and found the waters to be bitter and undrinkable, YHWH showed Moses a branch whereby the waters were miraculously cured of their curse. Thereupon follows a homily:

> If you truly listen to the voice of YHWH Your God
> and do that which is right in His eyes and give ear,

71

> then all of the sickness which I placed upon the
> Egyptians I will not place upon you. For I am
> YHWH—your curer. (Exod. 15:26)

The preacher is clearly referring to God's making the water and
food of the Egyptian unusable, the curse being the sickness and
the sickness the curse.

III. GOD THE DIVINE RATIONALIST

The insertion of the empirical, and therefore the rational, into
human-Divine relationships is illuminating. One aspect of this
rationality is the whole subject of testing. On the one hand, the
tests to which God subjects Abraham and Job have an element
of arbitrariness to them. The only proper human response—at
least at an earlier stage—was the humble acceptance of God's
plan. Furthermore, man is warned not to test God (Deut. 6:16).

On the other hand, we find a most remarkable passage in
Judges 6:36–40. Gideon has been elected by God to save Israel
from its enemies. Gideon, however, wants an almost empirical
assurance that his mission is indeed divinely instituted and that
it will be a success. To do this, he sets up a type of controlled
experiment. He places some fleece on the threshing floor and
makes the following conditions: if the fleece will be wet and the
ground dry, "then I will know for sure that victory will come."
Gideon demands of God that he be allowed to decide rationally
whether to sign on, and God rationally understands the demand
and agrees to let him do so.

Indeed, there is one whole class of omens, or 'otot (sing.,
'ot), that is actually used to demand of God evidence about events
in the future. Abraham's servant in Genesis 24, Gideon in Judges
6, and Jonathan in 1 Samuel 14 are all clear examples of this class.
The omen is spontaneous and was never incorporated into any institutionalized science of omens administrated by a special priestly

class, as was the case in Mesopotamia. Second, the omen was actually staged by the human being asking the questions. The servant of Abraham says: "Let the maiden to whom I say, 'Please, lower your jar that I may drink,' and who replies, 'Drink, and I will also water your camels'—let her be the one whom You have decreed for Your servant Israel. Thereby I shall know that You have dealt graciously with my master" (Gen. 24:14).

I do not think this was case in Mesopotamia.[9] There we are dealing with a science based on quasi-empirical observation of natural phenomena and their correlation with specific human mishaps or successes. If the sun was in a certain position on a specific day of the month and the army was defeated, then in future years battle was not to be attempted on that day. Furthermore, the omen had to be interpreted by the priest since it was usually ambiguous. I do not know of cases where a layman staged the conditions of his own omen so that by planning it, it would be completely clear and unambiguous.

The second type of *'ot* is the one used to authenticate a previous prophecy. This *'ot* can either be a natural portent, an earthquake or an eclipse of the sun, or as so often in the later prophets—a dramatic effectuation of the prophecy by means of a prophetic dumb show.

One of the most astounding features of the spontaneous omen is that a human being dictates the conditions of the sign rather than waiting for the Lord to provide His own. In Mesopotamia, when the king wants to determine the auspiciousness of a given moment, he sends a message to the omen priests, who then examine the stars and attempt to interpret their ambiguous and hidden message through the use of their occult quasi-empirical science. The number of significant portents is limited and completely stereotypical, as are the significant malformations of the liver of the sacrificial lamb, which were also used for divination.

This is not really true in Israel. When Jonathan wants to find out whether he is going to be successful or not, he sets up the conditions of the omen himself rather than waiting for God to create some portentous natural disturbance (1 Sam. 14:8–10). Moreover, the actual sign is quite simple and taken from the sphere of ordinary interpersonal actions, as is the omen the servant of Abraham sets up. This authenticating omen is the forerunner of the later prophetic *'ed* found in First Isaiah, Habakkuk, and Second Isaiah. God is sure that the cynical Jews will attribute the fulfillment of former prophecies either to fate (like the Philistine magicians, who have the same Jewish empirical approach) or to their idols. But they all share the distinctive belief that they may, to some extent, interact rationally with God, and in all these cases God apparently agrees and reacts rationally to their requests.

Nor is it only with favored individuals that God agrees to be tested in this way. Usually when God dispatches a prophet with a prophecy, in order to convince the doubting Thomases of His history-making powers and His ability to effectuate His prophecy, YHWH often informs the populace of some hocus-pocus *('ot* or *pele')* He will perform in a moment or He will ask them to ask for a sign. In effect, God is pulling rabbits out of His hat in order to convince an incredulous people that He really has the power to carry out His own prophecies.

Babylonian gods, in contrast, merely inform their servants, the kings—not the entire hoi polloi—of their prophecies, through dreams and other portents obfuscated by obscure symbolism.[10] In spite of the ambiguity of the message, they take it for granted that the king will fathom their command; the responsibility is all his and if he fails to ascertain their meaning even after subsequent portents, he will be punished for his lack of piety. Their gods are not interested in his enthusiasm or belief but rather in his immediate and complete obedience.

The situation is quite different in Israel. God first of all informs the whole people of His intentions and demands, in clear unequivocal language with minimal symbolism. Then He is concerned with their mental state; do they really believe in His creative powers? Instead of being angry at their typical lack of faith, He voluntarily offers to dispel their disbelief by a foretaste of His power, usually in the form of some magic that He often asks them to dictate. From the point of view of the more aristocratic gods of Mesopotamia, this is certainly playing up to the sympathies of the crowd. But this seems to be the case exactly; God not only wants Israel's obedience, He also wants their faith, love, affirmation, and enthusiasm. God is always afraid that even when He fulfills His word, Israel will consider it a coincidence rather than a product of the divine logos. Instead of being angry at their quasi-philosophical demand for empiric proof, He actually provides it in the form of the preprophecy authenticating omen that they themselves can actually choose. One is almost tempted to say that God delights in their doubt because it provides Him with another opportunity to empirically/experimentally/scientifically authenticate His being. Instead of being outraged by human doubt, He actually encourages it (cf. Isa. 7).

God, apparently, expects human beings to behave rationally when faced with evidence of divine qualities, and His own rationality about this interaction is expressed in an all-too-human disappointment when they fail to do so. To Jeremiah he declares:

> I thought [rather naively] that if I would only[11] adopt you[12] and grant you a goodly land, a desired inheritance, things universally desired; I thought—how wrong I was!—that you would call me "my father" never to defect again. But, contrary to my expectations, you threw me off as lightly as a woman throws off her lover! (Jer. 3:19–20)

One could not want a clearer example of a divine judgment on the interpersonal level. And yet, the Bible does not censor out such a passage. If it is philosophically difficult, it is humanly necessary. Compare Jeremiah 2:21:

> I planted you as a choice vine,
> All of it tested and guaranteed seed,
> How could you turn out so stinkily,
> An alien vine [one not expected]?

Shock after shock! What happened to divine omnipotence?

Similarly, though God does at times appear to be arbitrary in the use of His absolute power, this phenomenon has to be balanced with its opposite, reflected in divine self-justifications directed either to the sinners or obliquely to an imaginary audience; the theme of "What did I do wrong?" or "What did I not do that I should have?" so frequent in Jeremiah and the other prophets as well. The classic example is that of Isaiah 5, the allegory of the vine—a speech that must have had its effect on the young Jeremiah. Once upon a time, a man planted a vine in a field. He cleared it of stones and brambles, fenced it in, and provided it with a tower to protect it from the elements, man, and beast. He hoped for the choicest grapes, but disappointed asks: "What did I do?" or "What more could I have done?" (Isa. 5:4).

Another aspect of this underlying rationality is the argument that (1) it's just not natural; it doesn't make sense; or (2) it doesn't benefit you—you must be out of your mind to do things that are of no *use,* and that are against your best interest! Jeremiah is particularly rich in such rhetorical tropes. Look, says the prophet: Just look at the nations of the world. Did they ever exchange their gods—who are, after all, nothings—while my people exchange me for that which is without use! (Jer. 2:11). Can you think of anything more stupid than rejecting a spring of freshwater, for the brackish water of a cistern, a broken one! (Jer. 2:13). Or: You poor fools! Your shoes get worn out from running after foreign gods, and your voice has become parched from calling them. Do yourselves a favor, save your feet and be kind to your voice. And the people retort, Get off my back! I like my lovers! (Jer. 2:25).

A similar mode of argumentation based on the daring

image of God the midwife-obstetrician is found in Isaiah: "Will I induce labor pains and not carry out the birth successfully?" (66:9). Perish the thought! Such action doesn't make sense.

A god who uses a wide range of logical and rhetorical devices in an attempt to "get over" to his people, tacitly allows them—or many of them—to use the same devices in trying to convince Him. For example, with a version of the same midwife image, Job demands this kind of rational behavior from God:

> You invested in me so much creative energy.
> Your own hands made me and established me....
> Be mindful. How you shaped me like clay....
> Like milk you poured me out and like cheese you
>   congealed me.
> You invested me with skin and flesh
> And created in me a lattice work of bone and sinew
> You graciously granted me life and your concern for
>   me kept me alive.
> (Job 10:8–12)

"After all this effort, you want to kill me!?" Job asks, only half rhetorically. After all, "the days of my life are few and fleeting. Turn away from me. Call a halt to this behavior. Let me live! Let me catch my breath a bit, before I go, never to return, to a land of pitch black darkness" (cf. Job 10:20–21).

With the passage of Job in mind, the author of Psalm 119 argues: "Your hands made me and established me. Therefore ..." We expect something like "keep me alive" (119:17). But instead of physical life, this particular psalmist substitutes that something which gives spiritual life—namely *mitzvot*! You invested so much care in creating my body, you would deny me now that which keeps the soul alive!?

In the modern Near East and probably in the ancient Near East as well, it was not unusual for the same person who helped to midwife the birth of a child to later serve as a nanny, teaching the child his first steps and raising him. It was also not unusual for the same person to act as a maid or valet in the service of the same child as an adult. It is this image, I think, that underpins several Psalms. In Psalm 71:5–18, for instance, we read, "You have been my hope, O YHWH, from birth, My support from youth, the one who placed me on my mother's breast, who taught me from my youth, ... who led me to a healthy and virile middle age, whose kindness I unstintingly praised. After having brought me along so far, will you not lead me into ripe old age?" Not to do so would make no sense, would be a waste of creative energy![13] The whole thing is summed up quite nicely by Job's plea: "Hold precious/value the work of your hands—!" (Job 14:15).

In a similar line of reasoning, David Weiss Halivni[14] notes that while ancient Near Eastern law codes do not usually motivate their own specific laws, the Bible usually does.[15] God's motivating the law, with promises of the blessings of long life and prosperity for those who keep the commandment, leaves room for rationality, for argumentation, and for a give-and-take. Even though the Mishnah reverts to an unmotivated law, a good part of subsequent Jewish legal tradition prefers an approach that leaves room for human reaction and reasoning.

IV. GOD THE BENEFICENT KING

Divine love for men was not unknown in Mesopotamian religion, but in most cases the focus of the love was the king, not the common man, and even then that love was not stable. Dynastic stability was not a common thing in the ancient Near East. What happens in the Bible is simultaneous stabilization and democratization of divine love. God loves not a king but a whole people, not for a moment but for all time.

What I am suggesting now is something possibly less profound, more simple. In the ancient world, people were either governors or governees. At the top stood the father, or the paterfamilias, and underneath him stood everybody else—wife, firstborn son, the rest of the sons and daughters, the extended family, clients, servants, slaves (both house-born and bought) debtors, and assorted hangers-on. We usually think that the father's role is to exercise power and that the role of the underlings is simply that of service, but this is a distorted picture of social reality. Both parties had rights and obligations. The father was obliged to care for the good and general welfare of those under his control. He was not just a willful despot. Even though love cannot really be commanded, affection flowed in both directions. The father loved the family that loyally served him, and the family—wife, sons, servants—looked lovingly toward him in the expectation of his fatherly beneficence.

There were a limited number of actual governors to illustrate this role. The main ones are, of course, father to his children; husband to wife; master to his slaves; and king to his vassals and servitors; and the ultimate governor is God to His creatures. It's obvious what happened. Since all these metaphors of the governor functionally were equivalent, they were often substituted one for the other, as was their terminology of rights and obligations. Thus God is king, father, mother, husband, and master. It becomes obvious now that just as the father is no despot, so God is no tyrant.

Unfortunately, our understanding of the kingship of God has been distorted by our almost instinctual association of kingship to the despotic use of power. Nothing, however, could be farther from the truth. It is useful to see of what the ancient Near Eastern kings boasted as to their lasting achievements. In a Phoenician inscription of the eighth century BCE, King Kilamuwa praises himself in the following terms:[16]

> And I was a father to one, a mother to another
> and a brother to yet another....

I adopted the *muškabīm*[the sedentary population].
Their soul/attitude to me was like that of an orphan
toward its mother;

He who had never seen the face of sheep, I made
him the owner of a flock.

And he who had never seen the face of an ox, I made
him the owner of cattle and an owner of silver and
an owner of gold.

And the person who had never seen a shirt from his
youth, in my days was covered with linen.

In line with the sentiment in the first part of this inscription, it is significant that in the Bible both the human king and the Divine are called "the father of orphans and the judge of widows." Similarly, the psalmist says: "My father and mother abandoned me, but YHWH adopted me" (Ps. 27:10), just as Kilamuwa put it that "the soul of the *muškabīm* is like that of an orphan to his mother." Collectively, Israel can say, according to Second Isaiah, "Abraham has abandoned us, Jacob does not recognize us; Only you, O YHWH, are our Father" (Isa. 63:16). In other words, the patriarchs of Israel have abandoned their people who—as waifs—had been gathered in, and cared for, by the divine king-father.

To judge from the Bible and from Near Eastern royal inscriptions, West and East, kings prided themselves on not merely the number of lands they had conquered or temples they'd built, but that they had established prosperity in the land, internal security for its citizens, and justice for all. Each one of these principles can be illustrated by many examples. King Azatiwada of North Syria prides himself in his days that the population enjoyed satiety and delicious prosperity, and that civil conditions were so secure that "a woman could walk on the street unprotected, while doing her spinning [and nobody would bother her]."[17] This situation should be compared with that in Judges 5:6, "In the days of Yael, traffic on main highways came to an end and travelers were forced to take crooked roads, off the beaten track."

This stereotype of the king whose administration is benevolent and secures protection and prosperity for his people is found all over the Near East, including Egypt.[18] In Kilamuwa's inscription, cited above, the king threatens that if the commands of his stela are not obeyed, "May the *muškabīm* not honor the *ba'rīrīm* [the nonsedentary population]," implying that if the tenets of his administration were upheld, each element of the population would respect the other in perfect social harmony. Furthermore, it was felt both in the Bible and the Near East that the very physical presence of the prince ensured the natural fertility of the land as well as social and civic harmony and prosperity. At the same time, this civic role is intentional on the part of the ruler, human or divine. Thus, even as the human king establishes just prices for food and builds roads, bathhouses, and water supplies for his population, so God behaves toward His people. This is probably what underpins the psychology of the formula of the rabbinic blessing: "Praised are You O YHWH Our God, King of the Universe." As a king feeds the needy, so God feeds me. As a king clothes the naked, so God clothes me.

In this, the Rabbis are simply continuing the thought patterns of the Bible, where God the king is benign administrator of the universe. He administers *(yishpot)* the world justly *(be-ṣedek)*. According to Yehezkel Kaufmann, there is a cluster of psalms that usually contain the following elements: a declaration that YHWH is king; and a description of the natural power— sun, moon, stars, and so on—rejoicing over the fact that God is about to judge His world.[19] This judgment has less to do with a moral judgment of the world and its inhabitants than with His benign reestablishment of the cosmic order.[20]

81

NINE

POWER, LOVE, AND JUSTICE:

THE POSITIVE EXPRESSION OF

THE DIVINE WILL

KAUFMANN, HESCHEL, AND SPEISER

If the three *middot,* or divine aspects, of power, love, and justice are the three basic poles around which all human experience revolves, and if the Bible has portrayed the human situation in all its dimensions, three twentieth-century Jewish scholars—Yehezkel Kaufmann, Abraham J. Heschel, and Ephraim A. Speiser—can each be said to have grasped in his system one aspect of the organic whole called the Bible and helped bring one of these dimensions to light. Their efforts are not antithetical but complementary.[1]

Kaufmann reveals in all its depth the dimension of divine power.[2] If pagan religion entails the subjection of divinity to the tyranny of blind metadivine forces, the revolution of biblical thinking was the liberation of the divine from this tyranny and the intuitive affirmation of an absolute will (Kaufmann's words), free of all magical and natural limitations. It is not the positive expression of this will that is essential in Kaufmann's thinking but rather the liberation from cosmic coercion. The positive translation of the divine will into the specifically Jewish institutions of prophecy and election are mere accidents of history and do not really matter in a true (metaphysical, hence universalistic) interpretation of biblical religion. Kaufmann does not ask why the biblical God is just, for other gods were also just; nor does he ask why He loves man and is involved in his fate, for other gods also can care for man. His question is: Why is He free of all magical coercion and natural limitation?

Heschel (and also Moshe Maisels and I) asks an entirely different question.[3] The focus of our attention is the positive expression of divine power—not an indefinite potential, but a surge of feeling and desire, and an actual choice. This second school takes Kaufmann's conclusions for granted, but it assumes that the first truth, about divine power, is but a necessary foundation for the second, that of God's love of man and involvement in human life. Psychologically speaking, power is an absolute necessity for love, for without it, love becomes febrile, an escape rather than an overflowing of abundance. The gods of the pagans, who were not as yet in control of their own inner natures and who were slaves to external cosmic forces, were in no real position to become involved in a Divine-human dialogue.

But power and love alone are vague and incoherent; they lack the actuality, concreteness, and specificity of the here and now. The real embodiment of power and love, in their interrelatedness, is in the realm of law. Law is both a coercive mechanism—an assertion of power—as well as a loving consideration of the rights and the uniqueness of every human self. A law infused with love but without the teeth of power would not only be impotent to realize its noble aspirations; it would also be incapable of reaching "objective" decisions. A law of power that knew no love would lack the necessary sympathy needed to consider individual cases. Without such sympathy, the objective norms of the law book, armed with the power of the state, are often the fathers of the very injustices they attempt to prevent. It is in this area—of law, state, king, and justice—that Speiser has made his real contribution to biblical studies. He does not ask why the biblical God is powerful or kind but why He is just. Whether or not we agree with his answers, his question reveals the true focus of his interest.[4]

By way of summary, Kaufmann may be called the metaphysician of divine power, Heschel the psychologist of divine emotion, and Speiser the sociologist of divine justice. Each separately presents an incomplete picture of biblical thought; only in their complementary interplay do we get some idea of the full dynamic of the biblical experience. In a sense, the theological monism of the Bible breaks down into a triad of power, love, and justice, and these combine and interrelate with each other to form various types of value constructs.

ISAIAH, SECOND ISAIAH, AND JEREMIAH

Justice can combine with love alone and with power alone. When justice combines with love, the result is "creative justice." In His love for man and need for his sympathetic collaboration, God calls upon him to translate the divine norms into concrete reality, to assume the responsibility of moral partnership with Him. Every moral situation is a challenge to man's creative powers; his creative reaction is a loving response to the loving command of God. This notion is most typical of Jeremiah, for whom knowledge of YHWH is the creative imitation of the divine *middot:* "'Know that I YHWH do justice and mercy on earth, that this is the real knowledge of Me'" (cf. Jer. 9:23 and 22:15–16).

When justice combines with power, the result is judgment and condemnation. This notion is most typical of Isaiah, who stresses more than all the other prophets God's absolute transcendence, holiness, power, and otherness and man's ultimate fallibility and weakness. Before the utter exaltation of God's perfection, all human striving comes to nought. When the King, *Abir Yisrael,* arrives in His glory to judge the world, all human standards prove inadequate.

85

Justice addresses itself to the potential for moral grandeur that is immanent in man, but its demands can be overly heavy. When justice combined with power is about to destroy the world, a new configuration of *middot* makes itself manifest: power with love. This is the basic idea of Second Isaiah. Man has failed to live up to his potential, but God, in His absolute power, has mercy on him nevertheless. Justice recedes into the background.

God, in His love, forgives and in His power redeems. Israel is the passive witness of divine forgiveness and divine salvation. If Jeremiah symbolizes the moral optimism of normative Judaism, as expressed in the liturgy of the Sabbath and the festivals, and Isaiah represents the starker, more self-critical spirit of Yom Kippur, the spirit of Second Isaiah is most in evidence in the synagogue just after Tisha b'Av, when Jews commemorate the one national crisis in which human actions completely failed and only divine forgiveness and salvation could have any effect. On all other liturgical occasions, the Jew basks in the warmth of a creative partnership with God, drawing strength from divine reward; or, realizing humbly how far short of the divine standard his actual performance has fallen, actively seeks to renew the relationship and regain his standing. Only on rare occasions of national calamity does he throw himself completely upon the divine mercies.

This threefold typology in the prophetic literature casts some light on the attitudes of the various prophets toward intercessionary prayer. The creative justice of Jeremiah implies the relevance and power of human acts for the inner world of the Divine. Therefore Jeremiah is the intercessionary prophet par excellence. Isaiah, in contrast, never intercedes on behalf of Israel, for intercession implies love. If there is any activation of love, it is not man who brings it about but God Himself. Second Isaiah, on the other hand, does know of intercession: "I looked for a man who would intercede," he says, "and I found no one, so I myself represented the *raḥamim* (divine mercy)." This is most significant for a prophet who knows love but not creative justice.

In short, the prophets describe different faces of God, different attributes of the divine person. Each prophet sees and describes that set of traits most congenial to his own spirit. This is not to say that he creates his own image of the God; rather, each prophet sees what he can of the infinite spectrum of the divine self. In the last analysis, we are only capable of knowing that which is akin to ourselves. This is why it was necessary to send many prophets, of different emotional makeups: together, they enable us to fathom the Divine from many points of view.

JUDAISM, ISLAM, AND CHRISTIANITY

Christianity and Islam can also be more clearly understood against the background of this analysis. If Judaism was somehow able to balance these three elements in a creative but often uneasy harmony, Christianity and Islam each sundered the original triad, extracting one element and making it normative, often to the complete exclusion of the other two.

In Christianity, love became normative to the exclusion of justice and power. In Islam, power became normative to the exclusion of love and justice. One feels a decided lack of divine love in the Qur'an, as one feels a real lack of creative justice in the New Testament. For the latter to include a demand for justice that might be within human reach would have been an admission that man was sufficiently noble, in all his imperfection, to at least partly save himself by his own good deeds. This is certainly not the approach of Paul, and I am not sure whether it is even the approach of Jesus.

The Bible not only implies this inner tension but is actually able to concretize the idea mythically, in the demand that each prophet be prepared to stand in the breach, mediating between the divine demand for justice and the people's need for divine love.[5] The dynamic spectrum of divine emotion we are now positing is made even more explicit by the Midrash.

When the latter speaks of the conflict between *din* (justice) and *raḥamim* (mercy), it has actually personified these basic aspects of the divine life. It remained for the Zohar, which represents the culmination of biblical personalism, to develop the nuances of these polar traits and to describe the subtle interplay between them.

Ten

ON THE USES OF DIVINE POWER

The problem of a realistic relationship between the human and the Divine is exacerbated by the disparity between the omnipotence of God and the limited, if noble, capabilities of man. The problem is particularly fraught with tension in the case of the prophet, who is often pressed into distasteful missions by a divine being who seemingly lacks any alternative: God simply cannot go Himself. If force is needed, it is applied. But as we shall soon see, even the application of force is done with admirable delicacy and an acute awareness of the mentality of the prophet. Then, once the mission is accomplished and the prophet is suffering the aftereffects of having been coerced into something he could not have condoned as a "private citizen," God lovingly takes the time to explain His motives and, by evoking from the prophet a sympathetic understanding, relieves the pain of coercion. The prophet is helped in his effort to identify with God's position, to see that it was not arbitrary but based on a more realistic analysis than his own of the situation at hand and its concomitant demands.

To consider this subsequent explanation to the prophet merely a compensation for having coerced him would be to trivialize the divine intent. The explanation represents much more than this. Even though God needs obedient servants, He does not delight in servile yes-men who obey without understanding. He wants people of independent judgment who understand the reasons for His plan, the urgency of the situation, and the wisdom of the solution so that they can then be effective messengers, able to explain and expound God's words with intuition and sympathy. Their imagery is, after all, their own.

THE CASE OF SAMUEL

This whole dynamic is illustrated by the case of God and Samuel. God has just emerged from His disappointment over Saul and is, realistically enough, looking for a new king. In this, He needs the prophet's cooperation, but the latter, less realistic and more romantic than YHWH, cannot bring himself to take up the new mission. So he stalls, a most natural and understandable reaction. When YHWH scolds him—"How long are you going to mourn over Saul, seeing that even I have rejected him? Fill your horn with oil, and go to the house of Jesse, for I have picked out a candidate for kingship among his sons"—the prophet says, "If the king hears about it, he will kill me [for sedition]" (1 Sam. 16:1–2). No one who knows Samuel even superficially would suspect him, of all people, of cowardice. His answer is obviously a stalling technique.

But notice the cleverness and the delicacy of God's reaction. Had He so wished, He could have used force, saying, "I can see through your motives, you know. You aren't really afraid; you just don't agree with My plan. I tell you, I don't care what you think. I say you are going, and that's that!" However, this would have been quite a shabby way of treating a friend and devoted servant. It would have been just plain un-*menschlich*. First of all, when one is in control, it is unseemly to tell the other party to his face what the latter's real motives are; he knows only too well. To psychoanalyze him publicly, when the latter knows he will eventually have to give in, is enough to crush him—or at least to ruin his self-respect by taking away his means of saving face.

God doesn't do this. A prophet whose self-respect has been destroyed by the abuse of divine power is no good to himself, to Israel, or to God. Therefore, God plays along with the prophet's defenses. The latter acquiesces through the face-saving device of pushing ahead his scheduled visit to Bethlehem.

God has gotten what He needs from Samuel without destroying the latter's self-respect. But He still has not secured Samuel's sympathetic understanding of His moral position. This is important because the prophet's resentment against God will only increase if he is forced to act against his own scruples. Unless the issue is brought to the surface, the situation is liable to blow up. The prophet must learn God's reasons and assimilate the lesson of his mistake. God now uses His power, not to send the prophet to Israel, but to stage a situation for the prophet's own education. The staging has none of the artificiality of the Greek *deus ex machina,* for God works in subtler and more "natural" ways. He merely sees to it that David, the real candidate for kingship, is out tending his sheep when Samuel comes to select a king. Even though God has specified that the prophet "wait for further instruction," Samuel, still sentimentally involved with the image of Saul, jumps the gun and selects the tallest of Jesse's sons. Only now, after having made the obvious mistake of being impressed with looks instead of character, is Samuel chastised by God, and this time the chastisement is exactly to the point.

However, even here God is gentle, for there is no need to stick the knife in any deeper. In fact, Samuel is chastened more by the existential recognition of his mistake than by the divine rebuke, which is so much harder to face. One is always more prepared to learn from one's own errors than from the wisdom of others, particularly when this wisdom is moralistically and self-righteously conveyed. Knowing this, God does not preach to Samuel but rather sets him up to err; only then does He enunciate the principle, and the prophet assimilates it immediately. Unlike the hardening of Pharaoh's heart, which was an exercise in divine gamesmanship and an easy way to pick up some prestige using a despot for the fall guy, the divine staging of mistakes is used here for a much more human purpose.

THE CASE OF JONAH

God employs similar tactics in the case of Jonah, whom He clearly coerces. The fish trick is comparable to the *deus ex machina* of the Greeks. Jonah does his job, yet, significantly, the book does not end with the repentance of Nineveh but with the rehabilitation of the prophet. Once again, God uses His power to stage a situation in which the prophet will be experientially convinced of his mistake and of God's wisdom. Jonah says he wants to die. This is the typical reaction of the fanatic: either my ideals in their unsullied form or nothing, a most unrealistic position. But does Jonah really want to die or merely to be consoled? Why does God ask him whether he is put out unless he is, in fact, merely sulking? Jonah doesn't answer, or at least the text does not preserve his reply, probably because there isn't one, or at least not a real one.

Though God knows that Jonah doesn't really want to die, He does not shame him by telling him so. It is quite obvious from his joy over the gourd that Jonah still wants to live, even though he can't quite admit it to himself. What he really means by his protestation when the gourd dies is that he is fed up with God, not for having offended his principles, but for having taken away His life-giving protection. When God asks Jonah a second time whether he is grieved, He adds, "about the gourd," thus gently prodding Jonah to reveal his hidden thoughts. Our suspicions are confirmed. Jonah gives himself away: he really wants to live, and he really needs divine grace to do it. God has educated Jonah and instilled in him a sympathetic understanding of grace by creating just the situation needed for the prophet to realize the error of his ways.

DIVINE REALISM

When God created man He was very much like a doting father who expects too much from the limited potential of a very normal son; his expectations were not commensurate with the reality of the situation. Such utopian idealists are usually in for very great falls when their unrealistic hopes are dashed against the rocks of cruel reality. Then the realist gives up hope, repudiates the ideal, and becomes a cynic. This is essentially the Neibuhrian analysis and criticism of the rosy-spectacled utopian messianist who thinks that with a little bit of application, the End of Days is waiting to be realized in our time.

When God was suddenly confronted with the reality of human corruption at the time of Noah, His reaction was that of the shocked utopian, at which point God proceeded to destroy all of humanity except for the one "perfect" specimen He could find. As God found out later, even this solitary saint had his all-too-human weaknesses. During the forty days of the flood and its ghastly aftermath, God contemplated His decimated world and miscarried experiment and seems to have had second thoughts. Before the flood He had never realized man's potential for evil. However, once having learned about it, God realized that it was unreasonable to expect from man something that was not part of human nature. To punish humanity for not living up to an impossible standard in order to satisfy His own need for a utopian ethic suddenly seemed both unreasonable and even unjust to God. He then proceeded to adjust His utopian standard to the imperfect reality of man's nature as He now understood it. Better an imperfect man than no man at all, even if it meant compromising the purity and the absoluteness of His ideals. Life must go on; and without realistic compromises, life—idealistic life, that is—is altogether impossible. Only the orthodox and the fanatic seem oblivious to this most basic existential reality. God began as a metaidealist and became first a nihilistic cynic, then a tamed cynic, and finally a realistic idealist who learned the reality principle from his own mistakes and had the bravery to take another chance by making a realistic compromise.

What indeed was the compromise? The answer is as simple as it is profound: to suffer human sinfulness. A man who is not sinful, not fallible, is hardly human. Possibly God realized that if He is fallible in expecting the impossible from man and then punishing him, He had better have more sympathy for human mistakes.

From this, YHWH learned that if you want to make a fanatic more tolerant of the imperfections of other people, structure a situation in which the fanatic himself will make a tragic mistake and thus be in need of divine understanding. This is what the biblical God did in the cases of both Samuel and Jonah. In the Midrash, God has to "foul up" Hosea with a harlot to have him understand why He was ready to take Israel back.

In the Talmud, God already is armed with the foreknowledge of the biblical God and knows what He is getting Himself into; nevertheless, against the advice of the angels, the practical realists, He takes the calculated risk and actually creates man.[1] He knows what the angels are going to say after the debacle of the Tower of Babel; in fact, He had the answer already even before He created man. I am willing to suffer man's sinfulness, God says, to leave room for his humanity, for I cannot have my cake and eat it too: I cannot have a being free from sin who is also human. Rather a sinful human than no human at all.

Part III

AESTHETIC SENSIBILITY AND
RELIGIOUS IMAGINATION

Eleven

IMAGE AND IMAGINATION
IN THE BIBLE

RELIGIOUS POWER IN LITERARY IMAGE

It is commonly assumed that the spirit of monotheism in general and of Judaism in particular is antithetical to the artistic sensibility. However, while Jews may have been forbidden to make graven images, they were not forbidden to make literary ones. This is evident from even a superficial perusal of biblical literature. The Bible is not a collection of abstract dogmas but a full-blooded work of literature, a gallery of psychological depictions of the divine personality and His human image, man.

The image of God in the Bible is not a monolith; the divine persona is refracted through a wide range of personal prisms. Isaiah sees God as a city sophisticate; Ezekiel as a country bumpkin. As Yehezkel Kaufmann once remarked, it was a wise hand that directed the selection of which prophets were to be included in the canon. For, in spite of the similarity of general themes, each prophet, in his own style, captures different aspects of the divine person. And a true religionist should rejoice in the richness and diversity which source critics and tradition critics, often unwittingly, provide the religious sensibility. Thus, instead of having only one factual account of Sinai, we have a wide range of subjective reactions: one by the Picasso called D, one by the Rembrandt called J, one by the Blake called P. All these—with their thematic unity, their stylistic and intellectual diversity—are gathered up in that great library called the Hebrew Bible, which from the point of view of Greek antiquity could well be called the Israelite or Hebrew Anthology.

While the ancient Israelite was forbidden to make any plastic image of God, it would have been strange indeed if God, the source and creator of the human personality, did not Himself have real personhood. And if God is somehow a person, He must logically have a form that can be seen, even though it is insubstantial. Thus, Moses and the elders actually see the physical manifestation of YHWH sitting on a throne, supported by a dais of lapis lazuli. Similarly, Ezekiel sees YHWH as a man, sitting astride his movable throne made of fiery angelic beings. What profoundly shocking, mysterious images dance before our eyes, enough to stimulate and nourish the imaginations of a thousand painters and poets!

If the ancient Israelite did not himself paint the image of God on canvas, he did depict the divine image most graphically and concretely with the winged words of his religious poetry. The more monotheism repressed plastic representation of God and of man, the more daring and concrete were the modes of literary depiction. Thus, for example, in His relationship to sinful Israel, God compares Himself to a ferocious lion, a stealthy leopard, and a bereaved bear:

> So I am become like a lion to them.
> Like a leopard I lurk on the way;
> Like a bear robbed of her young I attack them
> And rip open the casing of their hearts. (Hos.
> 13:7–8)

Describing His nourishing treatment of the righteous, God calls Himself a fruitful tree:

> When I respond and look to Him,
> I become like a verdant cypress.
> Your fruit is provided by Me. (Hos. 14:9)

One would have thought that God or the prophet would have avoided such imagery because of its possible misleading similarity to that of idolatrous nature worship. But the image is not repressed. In Second Isaiah, the divine sense of urgency to bring about the delayed redemption of Israel from the Babylonian exile is expressed by the startling image of a woman giving birth:

> I have kept silent far too long,
> Kept still and restrained Myself;
> Now I will scream like a woman in labor.
> I will pant and I will gasp. (Isa. 42:14)

These few examples clearly illustrate the difference between cold philosophical abstractions concerning the nature of the ultimate principle and the graphic, concrete, image-laden mode of expression that is typical of the Hebrew Bible.

THE CHARACTER DEVELOPMENT OF GOD AND MAN

As Saul Lieberman, the great talmudist of the twentieth century, taught us, the truly tragic figure in the Bible is not Jacob or Saul or even Job, but God Himself, who is constantly torn between His love for Israel and His profound exasperation with them. God, who in the optimistic and almost naive glow of youth declares that the world is indeed "very good" (Gen. 1:31), is so profoundly depressed over the moral corruption of the man He has created that He says, "I regret having made them" (Gen. 6:7). How much cosmic agony there is in this divine attestation of failure! After having created the world, He drowns sinful mankind in a watery holocaust—and lives to regret it: "I will not continue to destroy the world on account of man, for man's instincts are evil from his youth" (Gen. 8:21).

The naiveté of God's original optimism and the depth of His subsequent pessimism are transmuted into what one may call divine realism. God now realizes that He cannot expect perfection from man and that human corruption is something He will have to make peace with. Man is not totally good, nor is he totally bad; he is simply human. God concludes that the appropriate reaction to man's sinfulness is not an outburst of punitive anger—His bow and arrow, which appear in nature as the rainbow, are permanently laid aside—but rather forbearance and an educational discipline in harmony with man's less-than-perfect nature.

In the first chapters of Genesis, God emerges before us as a moral personality who grows and learns through tragedy and experimentation to become a model for man. The crucial message is that even God makes mistakes and actually learns from them. This complicated, psychological being, this image in whose likeness man was created, becomes the model for the humanization of man. One wonders whether this psychological image is not too overwhelming for even the greatest graphic artist to depict. Only the literary theologians of the Bible, and especially those of the Talmud, seem adequate to the task. Unlike the Greek philosophers, who avoid the anthropomorphism employed by Homer in his depiction of the Greek gods, the Rabbis actually raise the intensity of anthropomorphism in their depiction of the complexities of the divine person.

Thus, for example, according to rabbinic tradition, the following dialogue took place between Moses and God after the sin of the Golden Calf: "Moses said to God, 'The Israelites have done You a great service in creating the Golden Calf. It will be

Your assistant. You will be in charge of the night; it will be in charge of the day. You will be in charge of the old folks; it will be in charge of the young folks. You will take care of rain; it will take care of dew.' God answered, 'How can you talk that way about the Golden Calf! Don't you realize it is a nonentity!' Moses replied, 'If it is a nonentity, what are You getting so excited about?'"[1] The divine anger has been reduced to an absurdum, to a joke, by the Socratic wisdom of Moses, who realizes most profoundly the depths of God's love for His people, a love that is occasionally masked by His justified indignation. Such vignettes are infinitely more humanizing than philosophical treatises on abstract morality. Here, indeed, the picture is worth a thousand words.

It is usually thought that what is new in the Bible is the abstract idea of God. However, what is really new is ancient Israel's understanding of what it means to be human, the idea that the human personality only realizes itself in its moral relationship with other personalities, whether of God or man. But instead of formulating this notion in the bloodless abstractions of theology, the ancient biblical thinkers intuited that the best vehicle for expressing it would be concrete and dramatic. Moral painting became a theological necessity. Hence the amazing literary images that gush forth ever new in the Bible: Abraham sacrificing his son, Jacob's moral struggles with himself and with God, King David's behavior in his youth and old age, and many others.

The development and growth we seem to see in the divine person is typical of human heroes, too, as they are depicted in the Bible. Thus, for example, the aged Jacob, who has suffered the rape of his daughter Dinah, the loss of his son Joseph, and other misfortunes, is very different from the struggling and striving opportunist of his youth. Jacob has grown before our eyes through the magic and literary skill of the ancient Israelite narrator. Similarly, in the book of Samuel a half-dozen Davids pass before our eyes: the young musician beloved by all, the fugitive fleeing from King Saul, the buccaneer fighting in the hire of the Philistines, the empire builder, the politician, the aged father crying over the death of his rebellious son Absalom. These powerful images of man have inspired artists, poets, and musicians of all generations.

But for all the concreteness of their depiction, the biblical writers do not tell everything. In fact, they seem to hint at hidden depths of personality, at unsolved problems, which draw readers of the Bible into their enterprise as active partners in a new kind of literary creation. Just as nature abhors a vacuum and God hates moral passivity, so it would seem that the biblical writers discourage intellectual passivity in their readers. This creative partnership between the authors of the biblical texts and engaged, responsive readers parallels the creative role of man in translating the moral script of the divine playwright into a living performance.

Imagine the following: the Shakespeare of all Shakespeares has created the play of all plays, the Torah, which encapsulates His program for the creation of the moral universe. He then tests a succession of actors, the ten generations from Adam to Noah and the ten generations from Noah to Abraham, to see who is best suited to translate His plan into concrete reality. He finally chooses a group of young actors, the family of Abraham, Isaac, and Jacob, and sends this troupe on the road for several generations—the wanderings of the patriarchs and the subjugation in Egypt. He finally makes a permanent contract with the company at Sinai. From now on the interpretation and execution of the play—the Torah—are to be in the hands of Israel. For the Supreme Artist, like the playwright or composer, is actually dependent on the artistry and independent interpretive skill of man, His creation.

Twelve

THEOLOGY AND POETICS

The aesthetic sensibility is not a matter of giving one's child piano lessons to make that child a better person. Rather, aestheticism is a total possession of the senses, as religion is a possession of the heart and science of the mind; if it does not necessarily make absolute demands on its initiated, it possesses them totally.

The aesthetic sensibility is first of all a sensuous appreciation of beauty. The refined enjoyment of beauty becomes for the aesthete an end in itself. Often this enjoyment provides an almost mystical release from the world. The tension between this conception and a religious attitude toward the world cannot be stressed too much. In the eyes of religion, any system that sets up enjoyment and delectation of the senses as an absolute good is creating idols. In the eyes of the aesthete, religion is puritanical and antithetical to life. The aesthetic experience, however, is much more than a hedonistic love of pleasure; it is also an attempt to relate the transcendent and the spiritual to the immediate and the libidinal. Think for a moment about our somewhat paradoxical reaction to stirring music. On the one hand, it is often the most spiritual of experiences; we are uplifted, even

103

illuminated. Yet, at the same time, it is the most physical of re-actions; our heart beats quicker and the music stirs not only our soul but our viscera as well. Thus, one can say that the aesthetic sensibility is a special mode of confronting reality in all its total immediacy with all the powers of the body and soul heightened at the moment of confrontation: the soul becomes clairvoyant and new heavens open up.

Whatever the theological stance of the aesthete, the aesthetic experience shares a vocabulary with the religious experience. The vision of the poet is not distant from the vision of the prophet; the experience of poetry is not removed from the experience of the Divine.

THE EXPERIENCE OF POETRY

There is something passive about the aesthete: he is not a creator but an enjoyer of beauty; he is a critic, a taster—a spectator; he wants to be entertained and excited. The poet, however, is the high priest of the aesthetic sensibility; his role is to create new value and new beauty in the world; he is the creative visionary who structures his experiences into works of lasting beauty.

From a structural point of view, the poet combines the best elements of the Buddhist, the Gnostic, and the Jew. Like the Buddhist and the Gnostic, he is a Promethean figure who balks against the limitations of the senses; but like the Jew, he affirms the goodness of existence. The poet is essentially a visionary who strives to penetrate the outer core of reality, to enter its holy of holies and to see reality in all its clarity and horror. To do this, he converts his being into a sensitive instrument capable of reacting to every nuance of reality, of every insight hidden in stereotyped words and everyday speech. He realizes ever so painfully that man is afraid of confronting existence in all of its grandeur and horror, and that words are more often used to block out reality instead of transmitting it. The palliative of words may be necessary for others, but not for him: he wants to feel directly, to see immediately, to strip words of their protective coverings in order to penetrate the very core of reality—to behold the vision of reality in all of its intensity. He is willing to pay the price for his daring: not all who throw away the accepted structures of vision return as illuminati; some return blind or go mad.

But unlike some mystics who are the passive aesthetes of the religious experience, contented with the excitation of their sensibilities, the poet—the godlike creator—feels himself coerced, obligated, by the immensity of the vision, to convert this oceanic feeling into a structure of permanence, a structure that sustains him in the moments of darkness that follow the vision, that allows him to communicate the message to other like-minded souls. If the truth must be told, the poet as a creator simply has the urge to create. Deep down in his heart he resents the fact that he was overwhelmed by the vision, and instead of remaining supine like the aesthete, in an act of Promethean rebellion, he converts the possession of the vision into the work of his hands. By converting the experience into a plastic form—by creating out of it—he becomes its god as well as its prophet.

THE POET AND LAW

At the moment when the poet attempts to come back into the world in order to create a poem out of his vision, he is faced with a remarkable paradox: the vision is boundless; it knows no laws; it is free-flowing spirit. And yet to create, the poet must pour the limitless into the mold of limit and form! Words are needed, yet the poet knows well the limitation of words: the very poetic experience was a (futile) attempt to transcend this limitation. Poetry needs measure and meter and cadence, and as a musical form must be well tempered. But measure and cadence are law in its purest form. To be a creator one must sacrifice the limitlessness of the insight to the dictates of reality: form and law. The poet, like God, is a spiritual realist who brings the spirit down to earth and structures it within the inner laws and limits of reality. The person who originally rejected words and their limits returns to these very words after having experienced the infinite, and with a magic touch refreshes and breathes into these words some of the experience he has just tasted. Without the periodic reshaping of words by the insights of poets, language and humanity would probably wither and die.

Poetry, in its attempt to combine the opposites—the limitless with the limited, the ineffable and the spoken, the spiritual and the libidinous—may seem to many as a paradox to be rejected, as an obfuscation of the mind, but upon further observation it is clear that poetry is the most meaningful model for human existence: only by bringing together these opposites, by bringing the spirit into the world through the instrument of the law, can life be redeemed from its emptiness. Although the poet is a mystic who resents the limitations of the senses, he is a Jew at heart—one who affirms the goodness of reality and creates new worlds of meaning out of the unformed clay of reality and human speech.

Finally, it should be noted that just as law is the holy instrument for God's creation of the physical world and man's moral re-creation of his inner being, so law—words and cadences—is the magic instrument of poetic creation. One who affirms reality sanctifies the law.

POETRY AND RELIGION

Every poem is a challenge to our total being: our senses, our intelligence, and our soul. We are afraid to confront the poem head-on (or at all) because we may be found lacking in the balance. Poems are written in a special language, and even though we instinctively know this, to defend ourselves, we dismiss poems as "only poetry." Thus, most people act in one of two ways: they either reject poems as silly or they read them literally. However, to read them literally is to overlook the fact that every poetic statement is a compromise between what is seen and what can be said in the limits of words. Poetry is by its very nature indeterminate; it is more exact than most human speech, but from the poet's point of view it is a kind of eloquent stammering. To take it literally is to overlook the essential paradox of the poetic art. However, poets make impossible demands on their readers: to understand what a poem is, one has to have experienced, in some way or another, the same exasperation with the emptiness of speech as it is commonly used, the attempt to transcend these limits by a total confrontation of reality with the powers of mind and soul, the creative urge to reshape this reality, and the impossibility of putting reality into words. The poet summons his reader to develop all these powers of being to meet the task of poetry. But such a summons makes too great a demand; therefore, people write prose instead, and when confronted by poetry, will immediately remove its sting and convert its evocative nondeterminate message into the clear and dogmatic—and often quite boring—catechism of responsible prose.

The structures of religion and poetry are quite similar: both the poet and the prophet break through to a realm of experience that is ultimately ineffable; both of them attempt the impossible by returning to the world of reality in order to announce the vision through the mediation of the word. Both attempt thereby to establish grounded on the earth a ladder whose head reaches to the heavens. In both cases, the actual message is a compromise: the infinite is encapsulated in the bounded; it is an inner paradox; it is indeterminate and radiates an aura of meaning; its spectrum cannot be easily defined, even though all who confront it are moved and come away enriched in some mysterious way. And both are a source of consternation for the masters of prose, who fear the wildness caught up in the capsules of words—the fire and the ecstasy and above all the momentary freedom. In their fear of this unknown and unexperienced reality, they modulate the intensity of the poem or the religious statement as it came forth from the prophet's mouth and convert it into manageable and proper structures. Poems are emasculated into prose and religion is converted into churches.

Who knows—maybe this is as it should be; maybe this is the inherent law of reality to which all, including the poet, should bow. After all, both poets and prophets are "possessed" and irresponsible, and society cannot long endure the intensity of their vision. Is it not significant that when God confronted all of Israel at Sinai, the people were overwhelmed by the intensity of the experience and were afraid that they would die? So they asked Moses to modulate the intensity of the experience by mediating between them and God. The fire had to be converted to human speech for the experiment to endure.

POETRY AND MIDRASH

Religion has to become institutionalized: this is the law of reality. However, institutions do not look with favor on spiritual individualists who depart from the norm to experience religion more immediately. And, as we have said, they are not altogether wrong: religious enthusiasm is often—especially in our day—a cover for insanity. Institutions impose a certain rationality on an essentially irrational phenomenon. However, if religion censures the religious enthusiast who wants to go it alone, it is also a bit suspicious of poets, especially of the poets and the enthusiasts whose revelations form the basis of the later institutions. And even if men like Moses did not fall on their faces in manic possession like some later prophets, and even though their confrontation with the Divine was through the "clear mirror" of speech rather than through the "dark mirror" of ecstasy, nevertheless Moses, after his encounter with the Divine, so reflected the divine fire that a mask had to be placed on his face lest the people be consumed at his glance! And as a mask was placed on the face of Moses, so masks have always been placed on the faces of all profound religious statements, which are often couched in an irresponsible, poetic, yet eternally evocative manner. We only allow those elements of the original tradition to filter through our consciousness that we are sure can be digested and assimilated. Thus, we also censor tradition, wittingly or not.

In the light of these observations, it becomes clear why the midrashic tradition has been given so little attention while the rational Halakhah stands at the head of the curriculum. The laws of sale are more immediately manageable than is envisioning the Holy One Blessed Be He putting on *tefillin*, of which it is written: "who is like unto My people Israel."

Yet the Rabbis certainly knew what they were doing when they divided their time between poetry and law, for these are the two indispensable poles of reality: rationality and feeling, form and freedom, outer action and inner reaction. However, to understand the Midrash—a good half of all rabbinic creativity— one must learn the poet's art; to do so, one must learn from general culture, which has developed modes of poetic analysis. Furthermore, and what is more difficult, one must acquire the poet's sensibilities; if we don't, we will throw away one of the precious keys that unlock the language of all true religious speech. Even though the Rabbis built a church on the foundations of law, and even though they said that scholars were preferable to prophets, they still retained the *bat qol* (heavenly voice) of revelation, the gift, of poetry. For what is not Halakhah in the Talmud is poetry—without rhyme and meter but poetry nevertheless. One who avoids it does so in fear; one who takes it literally is a fool. Midrash, like poetry, must be taken very seriously but not literally. It is therefore a challenge, and its language, although seemingly simple as a folktale, is more elusive than the complicated but straightforward dialectic of the law.

MIDRASH AND THEOLOGY

Those who say Judaism had no formal theology before the Middle Ages are probably right; all we have are legal statements that are binding and poetic statements about the world that, in the main, are not. Even though certain actions were made normative, the subjective reactions were not fixed: Midrash is the subjective, evocative, nondeterminate, personal reaction to the law. Theologies, on the other hand, are rational and clear—and as normative for belief as law is normative for action.

All theologies represent this attempt by rational persons of faith to remove the poetic sting and the subjective irresponsibility from the myths on which all religions are based. Poetry is converted into prose to render it acceptable and unthreatening to the common person who wants a catechism but not a challenge. The Rabbis, however, were true students of the prophets: if the prophets described God in terms of human experience, the Rabbis went even further in the humanization of the image and thus created a stumbling block for the semisophisticated and a source of never-ending joy for both the common folk and the true intellectual. Compared with the Midrash, the wildest statements of the Bible seem tame; compared with the Midrash, the Bible is prose. The Rabbis in the Midrash remythologized the Bible.

Remythologized, not demythologized. In thus heightening the poetic quality of the Bible and elaborating the human characteristics of the divine person who now studies and prays and makes marriages and cries over the destruction of the Temple, the Rabbis unwittingly created a third road of theology. Modern theologians are torn between literalists who naively accept the myths of religion at their face value, with all the absurdity that results from such literalizing, and the demythologizers who insist that the poetic covering of the myths must be stripped away and the essential moral philosophical content presented in a rational way. Both, however, are wrong. The literalist, although simpleminded, at least has respect for the power of the image; he reacts to the poetry but has little respect for the mind. On the other hand, the rationalist, with all his respect for the mind, does not seem to realize that the moral intuitions he wishes to preserve are organically related to the poetic formulation and that to kill the poetry is to murder its content. Furthermore, that which was said originally in an indeterminate manner and as a personal reaction is now made into an often self-righteous dogma, objective and normative for all. Moreover, that which was originally said obliquely, with a twinkle in the eye, with a touch of paradox and more than a grain of humor, is now said in a manner so solemn that it merits the name usually given to it—"dead" serious.

Laughter is one of God's greatest gifts to humanity. God Himself on occasion is said to laugh. Laughter prevents man from taking himself too seriously; from making himself or his theology or his science into a god. Laughter is the built-in protective against the religious orthodoxies of the Right and the secular idolatries of the Left. Reality is so illusive, so impossible to accommodate into any pat system, that one can either revolt against it in a Promethean manner by destroying the self or in a quiet manner by denying the problem—or accept it with a smile, with Shakespearian laughter.

People who are concerned with the root problems of religion, whatever answer they arrive at, are not atheists. Anyone who finds in his religious tradition constant excitement, a reservoir of insight, a vehicle for the most heartfelt truths of human existence, is certainly not an atheist. Anyone, moreover, who pushes his mind to the very limits of its reach and then feels confronted by mystery, who in his resentment wants to curse that seemingly demonic power that gave people minds sufficient to ask questions but not enough to answer them, thereby creating unending agony for the most humane of people without giving them a commensurate opiate; anyone who feels the pain of the human paradox and yet somehow manages to call up sufficient strength and bravery to overcome the paradox by the catharsis of laughter that is both an act of defiance against death and an affirmation of life—such a person may be called a believer.

And when this person humbly realizes that this mysterious strength is not his own creation but rather a gift—and a responsibility given to him by his parents and all preceding generations through the grace of some unknown One; and when he realizes that this One must mysteriously partake in personhood—for how could the differentiated ground of being grant so beautifully that which It has not and is antithetical to Its being—such a person is truly a believer.

Thirteen

TOWARD A PHENOMENOLOGY

OF THE SENSES

Aesthetics has several closely related components. On the one hand, it is a mode of understanding analogous to philosophy and science: it has a specific content and message. It attempts to understand a hidden reality and to communicate it, to preach in its name. From this point of view, the particular form of art is but a vehicle, a somewhat accidental body of a more real soul. It is as if the stone, the canvas, the notes are a painful but necessary boundary of the art. The mystic is usually just such a philosophical or noetic aesthete.

However, there is also a non-noetic aspect to the aesthetic, one that does not attempt to reveal a specific content or truth somehow latent in reality. Its nature is creative, plastic rather than revelatory. From the building blocks of the body—from the senses of movement, touch, sight, and sound—it exuberantly invents structures of play: contentless improvisations of the mind played on the keyboard of the senses. Unlike the noetic aesthete (the poet, the playwright), who is a prophet seized by the call of his god's revelation, the non-noetic aesthete (the musician) is dedicated to no specific content and to no master other than his own fertile inventiveness: he delights in ever new structures—his abstract and contentless ideas—for their own sake. In this respect, he is almost a theoretical mathematician creating new geometries. The notes of his composition are pure logical relations; they are formulae and equations of intellectual harmony and elegance in which one finds delight for their own sake; they are pure meaning, pure relatedness—the act of noition itself—free of any specific content.

And yet, there is a profound difference between the creative aesthete and the mathematician. Although both deal with pure inventiveness and form, they part company with respect to their attitudes toward the body. The mathematician is so radical that he strives not only for a contentless form, but for a bodiless form as well. For him, real lines and real circles have no body at all; they are totally logical abstractions. Such an attitude, however, is anathema to the creative aesthete; he may want a contentless form, but that form has a body, a real one in which he delights. It has real notes played on real, sensuous instruments, orchestrated not in one eternal and ever-present moment, but in the real continuum of sensuous time. Since it has a body, it has a real movement of which no abstraction can partake. Therefore, it is hard to conceive of a composer who would find greater delight in the unplayed composition lying inert on his desk than in the incarnate composition played by musicians before a live audience.

As Michael Polanyi has expressed it: mathematics is abstract music; music is sensual mathematics. And music is the wiser—and the more real: it integrates the best in man into one whole. At the moment of the most abstract human activity—pure cognition—the creator is also a human and sensuous being, fully aware of his physical reality in all its goodness. Paradoxically, the self-transcending act of cognition is achieved only through the instrument of a well-tempered body. What could be more mysterious than the phenomenon of disembodied notes emerging from a piece of dried gut tied tautly over a body of wood and glue! Why is it that the most sublime music speaks to our viscera as well as to our minds? One does not have to be a Freudian to realize the remarkable parallelism between the structure of music and the natural music of the body, with their alternations of highs and lows, sobs and silences, culminating in a silence beyond sound; their juxtaposition of two independent personalities, each with its own rhythm, yet integrated and in-termeshed, reaching the same destination at the same time de-spite having taken different but related roads. The wisdom of music over mathematics is the wisdom of a soul—the eternal music—incarnate in a real body, the only proper instrument for the playing of an eternal music.

Above, we distinguished between the cognitive-noetic aes-thete and the non-noetic demiurge-aesthete. The various art forms—poetry, drama, music, dance, painting, sculpture—all partake of these two types of orientations, each one, however, in a different way and with a different emphasis. Any form of writ-ing—the novel, drama, poetry—has a cognitive predisposition. It wants to convey a content, to share a vision—to preach. On the other hand, any form of music, and to some degree, dance as well, delights in sheer inventiveness, in the conjuring up of con-tentless forms composed of dancing sounds and movements. It celebrates the autonomy of the senses that build castles of form for their own delight.

However, this is not to say that writing does not know musicality, or that music and dance have no content or do not attempt on occasion to reveal a truth other than their own in-ventiveness. Writing knows musicality. Drama has more of it than prose. Poetry has more than drama. In fact, great poetry should be as musical in its use of pure sound as the most abstract music, and as exact in its expression of ideas and insight as the most rigorous prose. The paradox and power of poetry is its ability to be intellectually illuminating and musically exciting at one and the same time. It is a tour de force, the pulling off of this most unexpected trick, the wedding of two enemies: the nonsensory abstract content that insists its exactitude is a result of its abstraction, and the sensuous but contentless sound that insists its musicality is a result of its sensuousness and absence of content. The real tour de force is not merely the marrying of these opposites, but the actuality of getting them to work together more effectively in this strange tandem than in their former splendid isolation.

If words can be used musically, music can be revelatory of a vision and of a content. In fact, speaking historically, music has always been the vehicle either of mystics (e.g., the Pythagoreans) or of religions (e.g., Bach). Pure music is really an invention of the modern age. In fact, this "purification" of music from any specific vision does not seem to elicit from it a greater spontaneity and inventiveness. If writing and music epitomize the parameters of these two types of aesthetic, all other art forms—painting, sculpture, dance—fall somewhere in between. They are hybrids of musicality and meaning. The explication of this statement will be left for some other time.

All art, in spite of its abstract inventiveness and its relative freedom from specific content, is concrete and real, in that its building blocks are the human senses of rhythm, sight, hearing, touch. I think it not unreasonable to characterize these senses in terms of a greater sensuousness. The most sensuous of the senses are that of touch and the closely related senses of taste and smell, which do not play any role in formal art but are extremely important in the gustatory and amatory arts—personal art forms not to be overlooked in any discussion of the aesthetic.

Sight and hearing are more abstract, even though one "touches" with the eyes and "ingests" sounds with the ears. Yet hearing seems the more abstract of the two: one hears disembodied sounds, while one looks at concrete and incarnate objects. Painting and sculpture have real tangible bodies, while music does not have any real body at all. In painting and sculpture there is no difference between the ideal and the real: the real is what has been realized on the canvas. The ideal in the artist's mind is no longer of any consequence. However, this is not true of music. The score of the composer contains, albeit in short-hand, an ideal conception, particular performance being only a faulty approximation. The real music is somehow transcendent.

Now, there is something tragic in this fragmentation of a primal sensibility of the body into the discrete senses of touch, sight, and so on, and in their further polarization into more "spiritual" (sight and hearing) and "less spiritual" (touch, smell, and taste). It is as if the original but nonfragmented sensibility yearns for its primal unity: to unify "sight" with "hearing" and "sight-hearing" with "touch-taste." Art critics do this all the time when they interpret one sense in terms of another: the "rhythmics" (music) of the painting; the "color" of the sound; the "texture" (touch) of the music and of the painting. The case may be overstated: it is not the yearning for a primal unity of senses—this is a form of mystical nihilism. Rather, it is the yearning of each sense to fill a lack in its own perception. The various senses complement one another, as meaning finds sensuousness a complement to itself in the poetic arts.

PLAY AND MOVEMENT

As we have seen, play is an essential element of all art. Yet play is impossible without room for movement. A lack, a privation, is almost an essential precondition of creativity.

Until now we have juxtaposed arts that reveal a specific content and arts that invent pure forms, pure contentless meaning. The former is characterized by the written arts; the latter by mathematics and music. The latter is distinguished from the former by its greater appreciation of the sensual and the physical. For the sake of greater exactness, we should say sensual, not physical. For although the notes are played on physical instruments, they themselves have no real body: they are almost spiritual entities, yet not so abstract a spiritual entity that they can be equated with a mathematical abstraction.

A comparison with religion may be useful. There are three kinds of gods in religion: the holy statue; the Aristotelian abstraction; and the middle-ground, the monotheistic god, who has no physical body yet is no abstraction. He is neutrality non-incarnate. Aesthetically speaking, He is neither statue nor mathematical equation but a musical note—personal and real, yet nonphysical.

Each sense lacks some element of the primal unity, and this is the privation that leaves room for the aesthetic play of "seeing with the ears" and "touching with the eyes." And like all play, there is something self-transcendent in doing the impossible. That is one of the reasons we delight in—and need—art forms and their playfulness. Similarly, the severing of music and meaning creates a chasm—a mocking challenge to be overcome by the playful inventiveness of the poet. And is not the "tragic" bifurcation of man and woman just such a challenge and an opportunity for creative human sport? Love is also such a serious aesthetic game—as the poets have informed us.

ON PAINTING

Painting is a real challenge to the aesthete. It has, in some sense, more inherent limitations to overcome than the other arts. It is all thing, all body, and seemingly little transcendence. It is two dimensional and must simulate three-dimensionality; it is static and must simulate movement, and so on in respect to the other senses. Finally, it seems to be the most literal of the arts: it seems to depict things and convey meanings. It is not true art, pure abstraction, real musicality. And yet, these very limitations may be its source of greatness.

Yet painting, and to some degree sculpture as well, have a great affinity to a certain religious mentality. Painting has a quiet and a permanence that is lacking in music. Music is too nervous, too unstable, too lambent, too ambiguous—too much in need of human translators and listeners; too much a product of being-and-becoming and its inherent imperfection. Painting is the expression of an eternal truth, all of which is quietly present at any moment to be contemplated. Therefore, some religions, especially the historical ones, seem to have a greater affinity for music; others, for painting.

Certain philosophers have considered the perfect to be static; the imperfect, to be dynamic. Truth is not a process or an unfolding, it is an eternal and self-contained given. Furthermore, truth is not in need of assistants; it is self-sustaining. It does not need agents to translate it, at the most, it has devotees who worship it and meditate on its truth. This is the difference between music and painting: Bach needs men to redeem him from the ambiguity of his notes; he is not completely autonomous, nor can he be dispensed with once he is played by autonomous people. The relationship between composer and player is completely mutual. The opposite is true of painting.

On the one hand, the painter is completely autonomous: he or she needs no helpers or translators. The canvas is not a musical score in need of orchestration. One comes to contemplate its beauty and truth, not to complete it. And yet, once this canvas is completed, the intentions of the painter are of little significance. The painting that did not need outside help is now independent even of its creator. Painting, then, needs no translators—it simply has appreciators.

Part IV

JOY, LOVE, AND LITURGY

Fourteen

INTENT, VOLITION, AND THE ROOTS
OF RABBINIC PRAYER

THE LITERATURE OF THE ANCIENT NEAR EAST

Much has been written about the importance of intent and
volition in rabbinic piety. However, the spontaneous desire to
pray is not always present in the heart of the worshipper. We
know that in some cases the Rabbis would meditate before prayer
to put them in the right mood.[1] Or they might articulate in so
many words their desire to pray as God would have them pray—
with love and joy—asking God to favor them with a bit of assistance. On one level, all these prayers are late reflections of a
religious situation also found frequently in the Bible. Coaxing
the sinner who is on the verge of repenting, God says, "Take
one step and I will take you the rest of the way." Thus: "Return,
you backsliding children; I will heal your backslidings" (Jer. 3:22)
and "Return unto Me, and I will return unto you" (Mal. 3:7).

Three formulae are employed for this purpose in rabbinic
prayers:

- *Ve-ṭaher libbenu le-ʿovdekha be-ʾemet* (Purify our hearts to
serve You firmly/willingly).[2]

123

- *Takof 'et yiṣrenu lehishta'bed lakh* (Bend our will to become Your servants, that is, to serve You).[3]
- *Ten be-libbenu lehavin u-lehaskil* (Grant us/place in our hearts the understanding [to serve You]).[4]

The last formula is particularly interesting. Here, the stress is on the role of intelligence and understanding as prerequisites of proper prayer. Prayer is not antirational or irrational; it is something done with free will and God-given intelligence.

Interestingly, the rather paradoxical prayer to be granted the intelligence and ability to pray also has its roots in the devotional literature of the ancient Near East. One example is in the tomb inscription of Adad-guppi, the mother of Nabonidus. In the text of the inscription, we hear of the exemplary service to the gods, notably Sin, Ningal, Nusku, Sadarnunna, Shamash, Ishtar, and Adad, that distinguished Adad-guppi's life. She is, however, careful to credit Sin with having granted her the ability to worship:

> Out of his love for me who worships him and have laid hold of the hem of his garment, Sin, the king of all gods, did what he had not done before, had not granted to anybody else; he gave me [a woman] an exalted position and a name in the country. He added [to my life] many days [and] years of happiness and kept me alive from the time of Ashurbanipal, King of Assyria, to the 9th year of Nabonidus, King of Babylon, the son whom I bore, [i.e.] one hundred and four happy years [spent] in that piety which Sin, the king of all gods, has planted in my heart. My eyesight was good [to the end of my life], my hearing excellent, my hands and feet sound, my words well chosen, food and drink agreed with me, my health was fine, and my mind happy. I saw my great-great-grandchildren, up to the fourth generation, in good health and [thus] had my fill of old age.[5]

This noble sentiment, that all which came to Adad-guppi she owed to the gods, not excluding her reverence toward those same gods, is echoed in an inscription found on a monolith attributed to Adad-guppi's considerably more famous son, Nabonidus. He speaks, as kings must, on a national level: "You place religious awe of your great godhead in the heart of any country in which you desire to dwell and its foundation remains steadfast forever; you remove awe toward you from any country which you choose to destroy and you overthrow it forever."[6]

The idea that the country owes its religious identity to the grace of the gods is very old. The only proper response, given the nature of the metaphor, would be to worship the god in return, with willingness of spirit and wholeheartedness. Nabonidus rises to this occasion, declaring later in the same inscription:

> I built anew the Ehulhul, the temple of Sin, and completed this work. I [then] led in procession Sin, Ningal, Nusku, and Sadarnunna, from Shuanna [in Babylon], my royal city, and brought [them] in joy and happiness [into the temple], installing them on a permanent dais. I made abundant offerings before them and lavished gifts [on them].
>
> I filled Ehulhul with happiness and made its personnel rejoice.[7]

These terms of happiness are clearly part of a conventional lexicon of prayer, of which we find many later examples.

Far more beautiful is the prayer of Nebuchadnezzar to Marduk:

> Without you, Lord, what has existence? For the king you love, whose name you called and who pleases you—you advance his fame. You assign him a straightforward path. I am a prince you have favored, a creature of your

hands. You made me and entrusted to me the kingship over all the people. By your grace, O Lord, who provide for all of them, cause me to love your exalted rule. Let fear of your godhead be in my heart. Grant me what seems good to you; you will truly do what profits me.[8]

Here the king appeals to the god, almost pathetically, that fear and love be implanted in his heart. He certainly trusts in the god's benevolence, but he cannot expect this love or fear as a matter of course. He must pray for them.

From other inscriptions of the period of the neo-Babylonian Dynasty (625–539 BCE), we can see that the main idea in Nebuchadnezzar's prayer, that the ability to pray properly is itself a divine gift, was a current theological conception. Thus, by extension, Nebuchadnezzar refers in another inscription to the temples he has built in these terms: "The building of the cities of the gods and goddesses, which thing Marduk, the great lord, commanded me and made my heart willing [to do], in fear without ceasing I have accomplished."[9] The idea that he has acted both as a result of the god's command and out of the free will placed by the god in his heart echoes his prayer that we quoted above and also a Jewish prayer we have mentioned: "Purify our hearts to serve You willingly."

The identical idea can also be found in the following inscription credited to Nebuchadnezzar:

Now at that time, E-ur-iminanki, the ziggurat of Borsippa, which a former king had made and erected up to forty-two cubits but whose top he did not raise, since ancient days had been in ruins, and the channels to carry off its water were not in working order. Its bricks the rains and storms had crumbled; the burnt bricks of its outside covering were destroyed; [and] the bricks of its chambers had disintegrated. To restore it, the great Lord Marduk made my heart willing.[10]

This inscription is only clearly understood in light of the other. The fact that the god has granted his subject a willing heart is not the same as having commanded him to act. In fact, it is a much greater kindness since the subject is permitted to act freely or, as we might say, joyfully. The king may well be calling his god's attention to this fact when, upon completing the project, he prays: "O triumphant one, beloved of Marduk, joyfully behold with favor my work."[11] The idea that the gods put the proper spirit in the hearts of their worshippers is not necessarily limited to grand building projects; elsewhere this same king makes his point regarding the fish offerings he has arranged: "The fish as a festal offering for Marduk, that for a long time had not been done, my Lord Marduk put in my heart to reinstitute."[12]

Actually, Nebuchadnezzar was not the first neo-Babylonian king to use this idea in his prayers. His father Nabopolassar used these terms to describe the council of workmen he assembled to discuss the renovation of E-temen-anki, the ziggurat of Babylon: "By the commission of Ea, according to the advice of Marduk, by the will of Nebo and Nirba, in the great-heartedness which the god, my creator, created within me, in my great chamber, I called a council."[13]

To return to the king whose inscriptions started us off, the rest of our examples will be brought from the corpus of inscriptions of Nabonidus, the last native ruler of Babylonia, whose reign was from 555 to 539 BCE.[14] He seems to assume that piety is itself a gift from the gods, an idea we have also seen expressed in his mother's tomb inscription. Thus, in one place, he prays almost pathetically: "O Lord, what pleases you, let me do!"[15] How paradoxical for the ruler of an empire to pray neither for power nor for wealth but rather for divine aid in coming to identify his desires with divine will. Elsewhere he credits Shamash with instilling in him the correct will: "That which Shamash, the great Lord, permitted no other king, that granted he to me, the king, his reverential admirer, and transmitted it to me."[16]

The king is not a prophet; but the identification of his will with his god's makes it possible for him to declare that the god has granted him the unique ability to do the latter's will merely by doing his own. The idea that the reverent king is so rewarded may help us to understand this Nabonidian inscription: "May [this temple] bring the reverence of Sin, the Lord of the gods in heaven, into the heart of his people."[17] And elsewhere: "May the reverence of your great godhead be sunk into the heart of your people."[18] The prayer becomes even more touching later on in this same inscription, when the king prays, first on his own behalf and then on the behalf of his son, Belshazzar:

> And as for me, Nabonidus, King of Babylon, protect me from sins against your great godhead. Grant me long life. And as for my son, Belshazzar, my firstborn, the sprout of my heart, may the reverence of your great godhead be sunk into his heart. May he not become accustomed to sin, and may he benefit from all that life can offer.[19]

VOLITIONAL TERMS IN THE LITERATURE OF QUMRAN

Much has been written about the almost Calvinistic nature of the religion of the Covenanters of Qumran. In the *Manual of Discipline* and the *War of the Children of Light and the Children of Darkness,* man seems predestined to be either a saint or a sinner. The clear implication is that human beings are not free to choose. One would therefore expect the idea of intelligence, that faculty which enables man to make proper choices, to be absent or at least played down. But paradoxically, the Qumran worshipper constantly thanks God for endowing him with intelligence and entreats Him to complement the original gift with the knowledge and determination to serve Him as He wishes, with a willing spirit and a whole heart—in a word, *bi-nedavah*, voluntarily. When this happens, man becomes one with the angelic choir that continually praises God.[20]

The paradox is mitigated by the notion that the Qumran devotee, though predestined to be a saint, exercises intelligent choice within the limits of his predestination. Hence the constant use throughout the scrolls of terms of willingness, and particularly the term *nedavah*. In a sense, this term is the functional equivalent of the rabbinic terms *'ahavah* (love) and *simhah* (joy), and, indeed, in the rabbinic literature it is often associated with these terms. One modern author has observed: "By virtue of the grace given him, the author of the hymns worships God with a whole heart and a willing spirit, *bi-nedavah*, that is, of his own will and from the depths of his heart, and not under compulsion."[21]

Jacob Licht has shown that the very act of joining the group was a matter of free choice; no one entered it unwillingly.[22] Here he contrasts the practice of the Essenes, who, as recorded by Josephus, adopted children and raised them according to the doctrines of the group.[23] There is no mention in the literature of the *Yahad* (Qumran) that one could simply be born into the community. Furthermore, the verb *nadav* or *hit-naddev* is used to describe not only the original act of joining, but also the member's continued good standing in the group, which depended on an ongoing activation of his will.

The concept of *nedavah* is also attested to in the *War Scroll*.[24] Those who voluntarily take up arms in the eschatological conflict described there are called *'anshe nidvat milhamah*, "willing men of war," and *'atudei milhamah nedivei lev*, "men destined to fight a war voluntarily."[25]

The situation is not exactly the same in the liturgical poetry preserved in the Hymn Scroll. There, one Qumran poet joins together the two apparently contradictory notions of fate and will to produce a new concept, that one should accept his fate not only with resignation but also with alacrity. "Hurrying" is often the metaphor used to express freedom of will. Although the poet does not use the terminology of joy, the idea is similar. He writes:

> Hear ye sages, and declare your mind.[26]
> Hurry to be of firm spirit ...
> And revile not any just judgment,
> For all God's doings are just.[27]

The "mind," which the poet calls *da'at*, is elsewhere said to have been implanted by God in the heart of man:

> You have put understanding in his heart
> To open the source of knowledge [*da'at*]
> To all who [can] understand [it].[28]

In another passage, it is not God directly, but rather God directing fate who invests a person with the spirit of wisdom that allows him to praise God correctly:

> Thou causest a man's eternal fate
> With the spirits of wisdom [*da'at*]
> To praise Thy name joyfully in unison[29]
> And to tell Thy wonders before all Thy creation.[30]

The idea that the knowledge necessary to praise God properly is itself a divine gift is reflected elsewhere in the assertion that man's daily path cannot be straight unless God makes it so:

> And the way of man cannot be established
> But by the [help of the] spirit
> Which God created in him.[31]

For the Qumran liturgists, therefore, all is in God's hands, including the ability to worship Him properly, an activity which almost by definition calls for a freely willing spirit.

Of course, God does not instill the same wisdom in all men; another Qumran poet observes: *ve-gever me-'amito yaskil,* "a man may be wiser than his fellow,"[32] or even *ve-ruaḥ me-ruaḥ tigbar,* "one man's spirit might outdo another's."[33] On the other hand, the self-justifying idea seems to have been current that, if God does not dispense the same quantity of knowledge to all men, it is, not surprisingly, to the members of the Qumran sect that He does give it freely: "To Thy lowly servants Thou hast given wisdom."[34] Elsewhere we find, "For Thou hast informed Thy servant of the secret."[35] That this secret *(sod)* is properly to be identified with the knowledge *(da'at)* referred to above may be seen from another hymn—"Thou didst open in me knowledge [*da'at*], Thou didst enlighten me with the [a?] secret."[36]

All of these ideas—free will, God's planting of knowledge in the human heart, wholeheartedness, the secret, and so on—appear in a fragment of a poem preserved in the Hymn Scroll:

> And Thou dost desire the offering of Thine elect
> And dost hate evil.
> And Thou hast graced Thy servant
> With the spirit of knowledge [*ruaḥ de'ah*],
> To [enable him to] choose truth and justice
> And detest the path of evil.
> Thus will I give an offering
> And seek Thee with my heart,
> To gaze on the secrets of Thy wisdom.
> For this be from Thy hand,
> And against Thy will nothing would be.[37]

Fifteen

JOY IN THE LITURGY

According to Exodus 19:4–9, God does not order the Israelites to ready themselves for the theophany at Mount Sinai until they have accepted His offer to make them a holy nation. Thus, Israel's willingness to enter into the covenant is almost a prerequisite of the divine self-revelation. The volitional background of the covenant is brought out even more clearly by the *Mekhilta*. In its paraphrases of God's offer (Exod. 19:4–6), Moses's exhortations (Exod. 24:3), and the people's response (Exod. 17:8), the Midrash depicts the urgency with which God and Moses seek to elicit a positive response from the people.

At first, God encourages Israel to overcome the difficulties involved in accepting the Torah. Thus, to the verse "If you harken unto my voice ... you will be My private possession," the Midrash offers the following paraphrase: "Now take upon yourselves the obligation, though it is difficult, for all beginnings are difficult."[1]

Then God speaks in a more threatening tone: "'And Moses went and told the people all the words of YHWH' (Exod. 24:3)—if you accept the strictures of the Torah in joy, you will receive a reward; if not, you will receive punishment.

They accepted in joy."[2] In other words: you will receive the Torah whether you like it or not—willingly *(be-simḥah)* or under duress. If you accept it freely and responsibly, you will be rewarded for your action; if not, you will be punished for your stubbornness.

A final exhortation is made a moment before the actual promulgation of the Torah; to the verse "And Moses went down to the people and said to them" (Exod. 17:25), the *Mekhilta* comments: "Get yourselves ready to accept the kingdom of heaven *be-simḥah*."[3] The threat and exhortations do not seem to have been needed, for the people immediately respond to the divine invitation with one mind, or as the Midrash to Exodus 17:8 describes it: "They did not answer deceitfully [i.e., they meant what they said], nor did they consult with each other, but all of them in simultaneous agreement [*hishwu*] proclaimed, 'All that YHWH has commanded us, we shall do.'"[4] Almost the same clause—with the added term *be* (as in *be-simḥah*)—is used to describe the people's reaction to the actual revelation: "When they stood at Mount Sinai ready to accept the Torah, they were in simultaneous agreement [*hishwu*] to accept the kingdom of heaven with joy [*besimḥah*]; even more than this: they made each other guarantors [of its fulfillment]."[5]

JOY AND FEAR AT SINAI AND THE RED SEA

The volitional and legal overtones of the expression *be-simḥah* are supported by a number of independent considerations. First of all, the *Mekhilta's* expression *leqabbel malkhut shamayim be-simḥah* (to accept the kingdom of heaven with joy) is the functional parallel of the *Tanna de-Be Eliyahu's* phrase *qibbelu ʿol malkhut shamayim bi-nedavah* (they accepted the yoke of the kingdom of heaven with joy); both are expressions of voluntary activity.[6] Furthermore, if the phrase simply meant "they were happy to receive the gift," the clause which follows, "even more

134

than this: they made each other guarantors," would make little sense. However, if *simḥah* reflects the finality of the people's intention and the seriousness of their will to observe the Torah, the clause is its natural complement: they were so serious in their intention to accept the obligation that they concluded their pact with God with a list of guarantors who would secure its performance.

The parallel clauses "they did not answer deceitfully," "they did not consult with each other," and "they were in simultaneous agreement" all confirm the volitional implications of the term *simḥah*. The first clause indicates one aspect of intention: they were sincere. The second expression indicates the alacrity with which they translated their intention into action: they did not waste time with consultations but acted spontaneously. The third term, *hishwu*, is a synonym of *hiskimu* (they agreed) and is a clear indicator of mental activity. In the Aramaic papyri of Elephantine, it indicates the willingness of two parties to come to an amicable settlement. All of these lines of reasoning converge on one point: *simḥah* in this context is a state of mental and emotional willingness to accept an obligation, a willingness that expresses itself in unified, spontaneous, and immediate action.

There is one more historical occasion when Israel publicly accepts the yoke of the kingdom of heaven voluntarily: at the miraculous parting of the Reed Sea. This midrashic tradition is reflected in the liturgy of the Evening Service:

> And when His children saw His mighty acts, they acclaimed and praised His Name. Willingly [*be-raṣon*] they accepted upon themselves His kingship, as Moses and the children of Israel, in great joy [*be-simḥah rabbah*], lifted their voices in song, saying in unison: Who is like You, O YHWH?[7]

From a purely linguistic point of view, *be-simḥah rabbah* (in great joy) and *be-raṣon* (willingly) are virtual synonyms, as has been established from other examples of rabbinic exegesis. Furthermore, the expression *qibbelu ('ol) malkhut shamayim be-raṣon / be-simḥah rabbah* in the liturgy is the equivalent of *qibbelu malkhut shamayim be-simḥah* of the *Mekhilta* and *qibbelu ... bi-nedavah* of the *Tanna de-Be Eliyahu:* all three terms—*raṣon, simḥah,* and *nedavah*—express the spontaneity and willingness with which Israel accepted God's kingship at two important junctures in its history: at the Reed Sea and at Sinai.

From a simple reading of Scripture, these two incidents seem unconnected. Furthermore, the association of the incident at the Reed Sea with a religious moment of such import as "the acceptance of the kingship of heaven" seems rather strange. There is hardly any basis for this association in the scriptural text itself. However, the liturgy is filled not only with biblical echoes, but with rabbinic ones as well, many of them of an esoteric nature. Thus, according to esoteric rabbinic tradition, as reconstructed by Gershom Scholem and Saul Lieberman, the revelation at Sinai and the parting of the Reed Sea have much in common: the Tannaim argue over the question of which of these two places was the one at which the Song of the Sea was first sung.[8] Indeed, in this esoteric tradition, the real Song of the Sea was identical with the *Shi'ur Qomah,* which is also none other than the mystical song of the angels recorded in the *hekhalot* literature, the song of praise that the angels standing in God's presence sing to Him daily. This is the same song that Israel recited to Him either at the Reed Sea or at Sinai.[9] However, it should be pointed out that the high point of all three songs is the so-called *qedushah,* in which God's kingship is proclaimed. The technical term for this act of acclamation is none other than the expression *qibbelu 'aleihem 'ol malkhut shamayim.* Thus, according to the liturgy of the morning service:

The angels proclaim as King the name of the great King ... and they all take upon themselves the yoke of the kingdom of heaven one from the other, and give sanction to one another to hallow their Creator. In tranquil joy of spirit ... they all respond in unison and exclaim with awe [*be-yir'ah*].10

At Sinai, Israel accepts the yoke of heaven, not *be-yir'ah*, in fear, as do the angels, but rather *be-simḥah*, with joy and gladness. Like the angels, Israel's acclamation is in unison, but it is the result of a spontaneous inner harmony of minds and not the product of mutual consultation, as is the angels'. According to the liturgy, at the Reed Sea "they all accepted His kingship willingly [*be-raṣon*], while raising their voices in great joy [*be-simḥah rabbah*].11

Furthermore, the acceptance of the yoke of the kingdom of heaven is not something that happened only in the past or that only angels can do; according to the Talmud, the recitation of the *Shema'* is the moment in the service when Israel daily accepts the yoke of God's kingship.12 Significantly, in the oldest (pre-Christian) form of the liturgy, the *Shema'* was recited together with the Sinai Decalogue, which, as we have seen, was intimately associated with the mystical Song and the acceptance of the yoke of heaven.13 The only other mention of a historical acceptance of the kingdom of heaven is in the phrase *u-malkhuto be-raṣon qibbelu 'aleihem* (they gladly accepted His sovereignty), referring to the Song of the Sea.

Now, it is quite possible that the use of both the Decalogue and the Song of the Sea was simply a means of resolving the tannaitic argument about the exact moment when the mystical Song was recited; the liturgy thus incorporated both traditions. However, there is good evidence that originally the liturgy did not contain the clause *u-malkhuto be-raṣon* ... and that the acceptance of the yoke of heaven was celebrated by the recitation of the *Shema'* and the Decalogue. The question may then be asked: Why was the Song of the Sea added later?

At least two answers are forthcoming. There was a natural tendency to expand this particular section: first by the addition of the parallel tradition concerning the Song of the Sea; then, by the addition of the *qedushah*, which introduces mystical elements concerning the song of the angels; and, finally, with the *yoṣer* (benediction for the creation of light) of the *tefillah*, which compares the song of the angels to the praise Israel recites daily.

However, an alternate solution is also possible: Once the Decalogue was removed from the divine service because of "the arguments of the heretics," its function was taken over by the parallel declaration of God's kingship—the Song of the Sea. This would account for the latter's recitation in the introductory service as well for the frequency of its use both in the morning and evening services. Paradoxically, in the present form of the service, it is the yoke of God's kingship with which the Song of the Sea is most clearly associated, while this motif, although specifically associated with the *Shema'* in the halakhic tradition, is not clearly spelled out in the liturgy itself.

ALACRITY IN THE *AVODAH PIYYUTIM*

The use of *samaḥ* (rejoice) as meaning "to rush forth enthusiastically [to perform a religious action]" has its roots in the Hebrew of the Chronicler, is reflected in midrashic literature, and is crucial for the proper understanding of early paytanic descriptions of the avodah service of the Day of Atonement. In the official descriptions of this service in the Mishnah and Talmud, the verbs used to describe the passage of the high priest from one section of the Temple to another are pale and lifeless in the extreme: "he went," for example. However, when we turn to the descriptions in the *piyyutim*, we are confronted by a torrent of verbs of excited motion: *'aṣ* (to hurry), *ṭas* (to be swift; literally, to fly), *'af* (to fly), *gash* (to approach), *raṣ* (to run), and so on. It is only in these compositions that we feel the lively tempo with which the service was, or, better, had to be, performed. As Ibn Gabirol puts it, before one action was completed, another was begun.[14]

Whether this speed was simply a physical necessity (because so much had to be done in such a short time that things had to go swiftly), or whether it was done quickly so that the priest did not have time to let his mind wander from his sacred duties, or whether the alacrity was merely an expression of pious intent—whatever the case may be, it is only in *piyyutim* that this frenzy is actually spelled out. The absence of such descriptions from the official corpora does not necessarily imply that they were invented whole cloth by poetic imagination. On the contrary, Lieberman and others have pointed out that many an ancient tradition was preserved only in the *piyyutim*—or that the *piyyutim* indicates some tradition not in complete harmony with the official corpora.

Now, interspersed in these texts are a whole series of terms of joy—*das, 'alas, samaḥ,* and so forth—that simply connote quick action. There is no doubt that if the poet wanted to stress the speed of the avodah in acrostic, he needed many more terms of motion than were immediately available. However, in recruiting terms of joy to express alacrity, he was, again, not just fabricating usages. As we have seen, from Chronicles to tannaitic midrash, *samaḥ* is well attested as a verb meaning "to rush forward willingly and enthusiastically [to perform a religious action]." In almost all these cases, *samaḥ* refers both to alacrity and to inner intent. Once one term of joy indicating quick action was in existence, the exigencies of prosody could legitimately force other terms of joy to perform as verbs of quick action as well.

Once verbs of joy were used to describe lively priestly action by the ancient *paytanim* (liturgical poets)—and the *piyyutim* (poems) are now recognized as being much older than

originally thought—all later poets, both Sephardic and Ashke-
nazic, followed suit. The *piyyut Azkir Gevurot* of Yossi ben Yossi
is preserved in the prayer book of Rav Saadiah Gaon. The poem
is a lengthy acrostic, with each ten-line stanza devoted to one
letter of the alphabet. In it we find the alacrity with which the
high priest performed his rituals praised in these terms:

> He jumped [*qafaṣ*] and put them [the lots] on the two
> goats....
> He ran [*raṣ*] as was right for him to do, and collected
> the blood in a vessel.[15]

It is, however, another poem included by the Gaon in his prayer
book that makes clear the reason alacrity was so highly praised.
There was no question of any sort of ritual deadline. On the
contrary, if the priest's haste was in order to finish by a pre-
scribed time, there would be no metaphor at all—speed for the
sake of finishing on time is not a symbolic act. The alacrity sig-
nified the joy with which the act was done. In the anonymous
piyyut Atah Qonanta, which appears in the text between *Azkir
Gevurot* and Saadiah's own poem *Badonai Yiṣdiqu Veyoduhu,* we
find three lines in the last of the three acrostics:

> He hurried [*miher*] and took the cow's blood and
> sprinkled of it on the curtain before the ark, on the
> outside;
> He hastened [*nahaṣ*] and set down the cow's blood and
> took up the goat's blood and did with it as he had
> done with the cow's;
> He rejoiced [*sas*] and mixed the cow's blood with the
> goat's.[16]

It seems that the priest's haste was only an outward sign of his
joy—thus bringing him into compliance with a general rule we
have already discussed, that the enthusiasm of the donor is the

essential element in a sacrificial offering. Here, as elsewhere, the outward manifestation of joy is the speed with which the action is carried out. In the same poem, *Atah Qonanta,* joy is linked with fear of, and respect for, God and His commandments:

> He performed the commandment with fear and awe;
> and he checked himself for any obstruction to his
> immersion.
> He rejoiced [*sas*] at the opportunity to fulfill the
> commandment, and so he went down and
> immersed himself as he was commanded.[17]

A few lines later, joy is again equated with haste: "He then hurried [*miher*] to sanctify [wash] his hands and feet."[18]

In its turn, *Azkir Gevurot* can help shed light on another *piyyut.* In the former we read:

> They came early to remove the midnight ash [from
> the altar];
> They shoved each other while running up [*rasim*] the
> steps of the altar.[19]

This passage refers to the riotous dash to the altar that followed the institution of the lottery system in the Temple.[20] When another poet, Meshullam ben R. Kalonymos, describes the scene, he uses the metaphor of joy: "They rejoiced [*'alsu*][at the opportunity of possibly being chosen to] clear the altar [in the] first lottery."[21] This passage can shed light, in turn, on a term used in *Azkir Gevurot,* the verb *'alas:*

> He hurried [*'alas*] as an angel in his patterned linen
> trousers,
> A ready horseman, an angel of truth to those who sent
> him.[22]

In fact, Meshullam ben R. Kalonymos makes extensive use of the metaphor of alacrity to indicate wholehearted intent, using much clearer language than this. In the following passage, the high priest is praised, not only for having hurried, but actually for having run:

> He ran and placed it on the stand and slaughtered the
> goat ...
> He kicked up his heels and stood outside the
> curtain.[23]

The same poet introduces us to a new term for joy, *daṣ:*

> His goal could be described as the sun going out in all
> its power;
> In strength and joy [*daṣ*] he wrapped [himself] in the
> garments of his glory.[24]

Goldschmidt glosses this as meaning: "His face shone as if with sunlight because of his joy at having left the holy place in peace; he jumped vigorously, i.e., hurried, to change back into his own clothes."[25] This usage of *daṣ* in a metaphor of quick action has its roots in the Bible. Job's final discourse contains this phrase describing Leviathan: "In his neck abides strength, and dismay dances [*taduṣ*] before him."[26]

It is in a poem preserved in the ritual of certain German communities, *Asoḥe'aḥ Nifle'otekha,* that all these terms (and more) come together to indicate the identification of haste and joy with the willing spirit in which the avodah service was performed. Sometimes we hear the standard words in Hebrew for hurry and swift action: "He offered his sacrifice with mountain myrrh, He hurried [*hash*] and sped [*vayumhar*] to take up the blade,"[27] "He hastened [*miher*] to slaughter by drawing the blade and bringing it back."[28] Sometimes, as we already have seen, the idea is expressed, in terms of jumping: "He awoke particularly early and took it, as he had been commanded; He jumped [*qafaṣ*] to it as a man of swift action, and did not procrastinate."[29] Or: "He jumped [*qafaṣ*] and slaughtered it and collected its blood."[30] Sometimes, instead of jumping, the High Priest ran: "He ran [*raṣ*] and mixed it with the cow's blood."[31] Or: "He approached the goat while running [*bi-meruṣah*]."[32] In other places, the poet expresses this idea with more esoteric terms for hurrying: *ʿaṣ*,[33] *gash*,[34] *naḥaṣ*,[35] *zoraz*,[36] and so on.

More important, the way in which the act was performed is characterized in several places as joyful. Once the poet uses the word *daṣ:* "He rejoiced [*daṣ*] and washed [his hands and feet] and undressed and washed [his body]."[37] In another instance he expresses himself with the more usual words *sas* and *ṣahal:* "He rejoiced [*sas*] and washed [his hands and feet] and undressed with happiness [*be-ṣahalah*]."[38]

Thus, the priest's strenuous physical gestures of hastening, jumping, running, and hurrying are outward evidence of his inner emotional state of rejoicing in service to God.

Sixteen

LOVE AND ALACRITY IN OTHER LITURGIES

A WHOLE HEART IN PALESTINIAN LITURGICAL WORKS FROM THE GENIZAH

Not surprisingly, many of the ideas we have been discussing can be found in a variety of liturgies, both Jewish and Eastern Christian. The remnants of the Palestinian Jewish order of worship preserved in the Cairo Genizah are particularly rich in this area. An old Palestinian version of the blessing to be spoken before the recitation of the *Shema'* reads as follows:

> Blessed are You, O Lord our God, King of the universe, who has sanctified us by His commandments and commanded us regarding the reading of the *Shema'*, to declare Him King with a whole heart, to declare Him One with a good [i.e., willing] heart, and to worship Him with a willing spirit. Amen.[1]

Here, the intimate relationship between the whole heart and the whole spirit is evident. Elsewhere, we have seen the whole heart related to the metaphor of joy and love. In fact, the continuation

of the text, recited between the benediction and the *Shema‛* itself, makes this relationship evident:

> You have loved us with an everlasting love [*'ahavat 'olam*].
> Give us to keep, to do, to study, and to fulfill all the
> words of the study of Your Torah in love [*be'ahavah*].
> Enlighten our eyes in Your Torah. Cause our heart to
> cleave to Your worship in truth; and we will declare
> You One with fear and awe. Blessed are You, who
> chooses His people Israel. Amen.[2]

Here, *'ahavah* is parallel to truth, fear, and awe.

The whole heart also has its parallel in other prayers native to the Land of Israel. It is recorded that the followers of R.
Yannai used to rule that one who awakens from his sleep must
say the following:

> Blessed are You, O Lord, who awakens the dead. My
> Lord, I have sinned against You. May it be Your will, O
> Lord, my God, that You give me a good heart, a good
> portion, a good inclination, a good outlook, a good
> name, a good eye, a good soul, a humble soul, and a
> humble spirit. Let Your name not be profaned by us,
> and cause us not to have recourse to the gifts of man, ...
> and place our portion in Your Torah with those who
> do Your will.[3]

This certainly recalls the willing heart of the benediction to be
recited before the reading of the *Shema‛* in the old Palestinian
rite we have seen above. It also recalls the statement of *Avot* that
the just path for a man to follow is that of the *'ayin ṭovah*, the
good eye.[4] And it recalls the familiar *vetaher libbenu*, "and purify our hearts," in the Sabbath liturgy.[5]

The whole heart is also the culminating image in the
prayer of R. Tanhum bar Scholasticus:

> May it be Your will, O Lord, my God and God of my
> fathers, that You break and destroy the yoke of the evil
> inclination from our hearts, for thus were we created
> by You, to do Your will, and we must [therefore] do
> Your will. You desire this, and we desire it. And who
> can hold back the leaven in the dough? It is known and
> clear to You that we do not have the strength to over-
> come [the evil inclination]. Therefore, may it be Your
> will, O Lord, my God and God of my fathers, that You
> destroy it from us and defeat it, and [then] we will do
> Your will as our will with a whole heart.[6]

Although we may never know precisely who this R. Tanhum
was, it is possible that he had some connection with R. Alexan-
dri, the second-generation Palestinian *Amora,* whose own private meditation following prayer—which is strikingly similar to
R. Tanhum's—is recorded in a Babylonian source. His prayer is
as follows:

> Lord of the Universe! It is known and clear before You
> that it is our will to do Your will, and who can hold
> back the leaven that is in the dough or the oppression
> of the gentiles? May it be Your will that You save us
> from their hand, and we will return to doing the laws
> that reflect Your will, with a whole heart.[7]

The oldest manuscripts record a version of the text that is even
closer to the prayer of R. Tanhum.[8] Clearly, the emphasis on the
heart is comprehensible above a mere homiletical level in the
greater sense of the term, where it is allied with its sister terms:
simḥah (joy) and *'ahavah* (love).

Few liturgical sources define the metaphor more clearly
than the *'Amidah* for Sabbath afternoon, where the link is
menuḥat 'ahavah u-nedavah, "rest of love and free will";[9] that
is, Sabbath rest is offered to God as a type of free will offering.

That this is legally required to be offered *be-'ahavah* is apparent both from the parallel liturgy for the Sabbath *musaf* service, where the sacrifices are recalled as having been offered according to specified ritual and legal specifications *(ke-sidram u-ke-hilkhatam)* and with love *(be-'ahavah)*,[10] and from the precise equation of the two (Sabbath rest and free will) in the special paragraph inserted in the Grace after Meals on the Sabbath, where we find the phrase "Be pleased ... to fortify us in the performance of Your commandments ... that we may rest thereon in love in accordance with the precept of thy will."[11]

The identification, finally, of God's will with the act done spontaneously and lovingly is found in an old prayer to be said at the ceremony while sanctifying the new moon. There, we find the sun and the moon praised because they perform God's will in joy and gladness.[12] We have seen above the larger metaphoric context into which it is necessary to inject this idea of the willingness of the celestial bodies to perform their assigned tasks.

LOVE AND WILL IN THE EASTERN CHURCHES

It is interesting that the metaphor with which we are dealing was by no means exclusively Jewish; on the contrary, it was so much a part of the literary atmosphere of the ancient Near East that it found its way into the liturgies of several Eastern churches. According to the Syrian Jacobite tradition, the priest before the Gospel prays thus:

> Grant us, o Lord God, the knowledge of thy divine words and fill us with the understanding of thine holy Gospel and the riches of thy divine gifts and the indwelling of thine Holy Spirit and give us with joy to keep thy commandments and accomplish them and fulfil [*sic*] thy will and to be accounted worthy of the

blessings and the mercies that are from thee now and at all times.[13]

As if entering into a midrashic dialectic, the rite of the Greco-Russian church, in its prayer before the Gospel, uses not love but fear as its metaphoric basis:

> O Lord and lover of men; illumine our hearts with the pure light of Thy Divine knowledge, and open the eyes of our understanding that we may comprehend the precepts of Thy Gospel. Implant in us likewise the fear of Thy blessed commandments.[14]

Another prayer from that rite combines the two ideas:

> Grant that they may at all times serve thee blamelessly in fear and love and that they may in innocence partake of the Holy Mysteries.[15]

Thus we can see the pervasive use of the term *love* in the liturgies of various rites where we would expect to find such a metaphor. It is, however, only in the context of the rest of the texts we have seen that its true meaning becomes clear. Love is the opposite of fear, not only metaphysically, but also legally and ritually. The prayer must be offered with fear—with respect—but also with love: with a whole, calm heart and with a willing spirit.[16]

Seventeen

THE PRIESTLY BENEDICTION

Considering the importance of the Priestly Benediction and the attention devoted to the details of its performance, little has been said about its religious underpinnings. In the few aggadic passages that have come down to us on this subject, God seems to be faced with a rather delicate problem. His priests are less than enthusiastic about having to bless the people. They reveal their resentment by insisting on reciprocity: after pronouncing the blessing, they say, "Now that we have done what You wanted, do what we want!"[1] They also make the (false) assumption that the blessing could not have been too important in His eyes if He elected to delegate it to human servants.[2] The Israelites, on the other hand, perhaps sensing the attitude of the priests, are somewhat offended that YHWH Himself does not pronounce the blessing. So God adopts a two-pronged tactic: to convince the Israelites that even though it is the priests who are uttering the formula, He Himself is actually blessing the people; and to warn the priests that they must treat their task with utmost seriousness, blessing the people wholeheartedly and clearheadedly, for only a blessing that is bestowed with love is considered worthy of conveying God's gift of love.

151

WHY DOESN'T GOD BLESS US DIRECTLY?

According to a midrash, until the time of Abraham all blessings were offered by God directly. Commenting on Genesis 12:2, it states:

> "And be a blessing"—but was it not earlier written, "And I will bless you" (Gen. 12:2)? [This being so,] what does the Torah mean to teach us with the [additional] expression "and be a blessing"? Rabbi Eliezer said: The Holy One, blessed be He, said to [Abraham], "From the time I created My universe until now, I have had to bless My creatures, as it is written, 'And God blessed them' (Gen. 1:28), and 'God blessed Noah and his sons' (Gen. 9:1). But from now on, the blessings are passed on to you, so that those who please you, you may bless, and they will be blessed. Nonetheless, Abraham did not bless Isaac ... and thus it is written: "And it came to pass, after the death of Abraham, that God blessed Isaac his son" (Gen. 25:11). And Isaac blessed Jacob, and Jacob blessed the twelve tribes, as it is written: "All these are the twelve tribes of Israel, and this is what their father said to them when he blessed them" (Gen. 49:28). From now on, said the Holy One, blessed be He, the blessings are passed on to you; the priests will bless My children. Just as I said to Abraham, their father, "and be a blessing," so it is said, "In this way you shall bless." (Num. 6:23)[3]

Why does God delegate the task of blessing the people? In a passage in *Tanhuma* we find God explaining to Abraham why He is passing along to him the right to bless the people:

> It does not suit My dignity that I should have to bless My creatures [Myself]. Rather, I am handing the bless-

ings over to Abraham and to his progeny, and so, whosoever they bless, I will back up his blessing, as it is written: "and be a blessing." (Gen. 12:2)[4]

In his book *The World of the Aggadah* (Hebrew), A. A. Halevi quotes several Jewish and Hellenistic sources according to which significant acts performed by God are eternally effective, while those done by men have less than permanent effects. Thus the Midrash:

> The Holy One, blessed be He, said, "In this world you were delivered by human beings: in Egypt, by Moses and Aaron; in the days of Sisera, by Barak and Deborah.... And since they were only flesh and blood, you were returned to subjugation time after time. However, in the world to come, I Myself will redeem you, as Scripture says: "Israel has won through YHWH triumph everlasting." (Isa. 45:17)[5]

With divine foresight God commands men to carry out certain actions—such as building sanctuaries and conquering enemies—because He knows that the people will eventually sin. Blessings originally granted by men can be canceled; if they are granted by God, they must continue throughout eternity. Thus, rather than tying His own divine hands, God leaves Himself the option of withdrawing the blessing.[6]

Whatever God's precise reasons for commanding the priests to transmit His blessings to the people, the situation leads to hard feelings on the part of both the priests and the Israelites. Thus we find Israel not at all eager to receive God's blessing through the priests. In a midrash we read:

> At the time when the Holy One, blessed be He, said to Aaron and his sons, "In this way you shall bless" (Num. 6:23), Israel said before the Holy One, blessed be He,

"Master of the Universe, You have told the priests to bless us, but all we require is Your blessing, and to be blessed from Your mouth, as it is written, 'Look forth from Thy holy habitation, from heaven' (Deut. 26:15)." The Holy One, blessed be He, said to them, "Although I have asked the priests to bless you, I shall stand with them and bless you [as well]." This is why the priests spread out their hands, as if to say that the Holy one, blessed be He, is standing behind them. Therefore, it is written, "He looks in through the windows" (Songs 2:9)—from between the hands of the priests. "He peers through the lattice" (Songs 2:9)—from between the priests' fingers.[7]

In another text, God seeks to calm Israel by promising that the practice of transmitting divine blessings via the priests is only a temporary one and that eventually the situation will change; God will bless His people in person. There, in a midrash on Numbers 7:12, it is written:

And it came to pass, [on the day that Moses had made an end of setting up the tabernacle]—The Holy One, blessed be He, said, "In this world, I commanded Aaron and his sons to bless them, but in the future, I, in My glory, will bless them, as it is written, 'YHWH bless thee out of Zion; even He that made heaven and earth.'" (Ps. 134:3)[8]

In His mercy God promises that, in the world to come, He will again bless man personally, since the new Israel will be free from sin.

THE ROLE OF THE PRIEST

The implied reluctance on the part of Israel to be blessed by the priests is paralleled by a similarly implied reluctance on the part of the priests to bless the people. Thus, in an old comment on Numbers 6:27 ("and I will bless them") we find this statement:

> One might think that only if the priests desire to bless Israel they would be blessed, and if not, then they would not be blessed. Therefore Scripture teaches: "and I will bless them" (Num. 6:27)—whether the priests do or do not desire, I will bless them [Israel] from heaven.[9]

Although this midrash implies reassurance that any underlying or overt reluctance on the part of the priests will not affect the efficacy of the blessing, other sources go further and portray God as forbidding the priests to begrudge the people their blessing. In one collection, we find this comment on Numbers 6:23, based on the plene spelling of *'amor:*

> "In this way you shall bless" (Num. 6:23)—Speak ['amor] to them [using the *plene* spelling], thus meaning: Say to them, to the priests, that just because I have told you to bless the people Israel, this does not imply that you may bless them begrudgingly or hastily [be-angaria u-vi-vehilut]; rather, you should bless them wholeheartedly, so that the blessings have power for them; and thus is it written 'amor lahem, using the plene spelling.[10]

What is more, the priests must carry out their task in a positive spirit. For this, we have the liturgical evidence of the benediction that is to be recited by the priests before they bless the people. In a sole midrashic source, we find this:

What benediction do [the priests] say? " ... Who has sanctified us with the sanctity of Aaron and has commanded us to bless His people Israel in love [be-'ahavah, i.e., freely]." And when the priest first moves to ascend to the platform [dukhan], what does he say? "May it be Your will, O Lord, our God, that this blessing, with which You have commanded us to bless Your people Israel should be free of obstacle or sin." And when he completes the blessing and turns his face from the congregation, what does he say? "Lord of the Universe, we have done that which You have decreed for us to do; now do for us that which You have promised."[11]

Ultimately, the relationship between the priests and the people, too, must be a reciprocal one: not only must the priests bless the people wholeheartedly; the people must accept their blessing wholeheartedly as well. One place where we find both ideas expressed together is in the Zohar, where the verb used is *rhm*—the zoharic equivalent of *ahb*. There we find the statement:

It was taught: Any [priest] who is not beloved by the people or who does not love the people may not spread forth his hands to bless the people, as it is written, "He who has a bountiful eye shall be blessed" (Prov. 22:9). Do not read it "shall be blessed" [yevorakh] but "shall bless" [yevarekh].[12]

If there is no opening of the heart in both directions, the benediction cannot be properly recited.

PART V

ENCOUNTERING THE PERSONHOOD
OF GOD

Eighteen

GOD AND THE WORLD

In the past, most religions considered the dimension of the secular—the world with its pain and imperfection, its pleasures and seductions—as an impediment to the attainment of godliness. In our day, as a reaction to this antiworldliness, there has been an equally unhealthy tendency for many religionists to lose themselves almost totally in the world and in worldliness. Others, among them many raised in the Jewish tradition, believe that the world is neither enemy nor end-in-itself, but the necessary, and potentially holy, milieu in which the spirit realizes itself, in which it takes form. However, even for these people, the inescapability of pain and death, the finiteness of our intelligence, the conflicts of our inner life are inexplicable and perplexing phenomena that often outrage our deepest sensibilities. Even for them, the physical world poses a grave problem.

Nor is it only material reality that poses a problem for religion. Secular society, with its cultural values, science, and aesthetics—independent of religion and often inimical to it— may present an equally formidable challenge. The spirit not only has to defend itself from the attacks of the scientific mind and the aesthetic sensibility, it also has to justify the existence of the

159

scientific mind and the aesthetic sensibility within the divine economy. If the mind destroys faith, and even the belief in the self, why was it created? Why does the "beautiful" coexist with the "good" as a possible, and idolatrous, object of man's ultimate loyalties? To put it simply: "worldliness" is often as great a problem to religion as "the world." This is especially true of the religious Jew, who may on occasion make his peace with the physical world but has rarely done so with the values of non-Jewish society.

In this and the following chapters, the painful but often creative conflict between religion and the world, the holy and the profane, the spiritual order and the secular one—whatever particular antinomy is preferred—will be explored.[1]

SOME PHILOSOPHICAL REFLECTIONS

Before we begin to consider a Judaic approach to the conflict between the spirit and the world, in the next chapter, a more precise definition of these polar terms is in order. This is especially true of the term *spirit,* which is often used as a virtual synonym for the terms *soul, the holy,* and even *God.*

It is assumed here that man is more than his body; that he has an objective psychic life; furthermore, that his psychic life is at least as structured as his physical life; that one area of this life of the psyche is what traditional religion calls the soul. The term is not used here in the manner of psychologists, religionists, or philosophers, but in the commonsense fashion often employed by writers and artists. We all know what is meant by the expression "he has soul." It is an objective personality trait; a certain kind of sensitivity, an openness to people and things, an awareness of certain dimensions of life, especially of the holy and the spiritual. We hypostatize this quality and talk about "the soul." Metaphorically speaking, it is one organ of the psychic body. It is an organ attuned to, and in need of, the higher dimensions of reality, the holy, and the spiritual. Thus defined, the soul is the subject of the religious life.

The spirit is that creative potential in man—and according to some, in nature as well—that makes for self-transcendence. It is the power that makes works of art more than the sum of their parts, symphonies more than the totality of their notes. It is that which allows us to say that the mind "creates" reality, not vice versa. Because of the workings of the spirit, sound becomes language; individuals produce and participate in collective patterns of culture; ideas are born and find expression in the symbolic forms of art, religion, and philosophy. The spirit is a power that is itself transcendent (it seems not to be derived from any prior category of existence) and that makes for self-transcendence in man.

When we say that the creation is sometimes greater than the creator, or that the creator, through the creative act, becomes more than he was or creates himself anew, we are confronted with a manifestation of the spirit, that is, of self-transcendence. One does not have to identify the spirit with God or even posit its origins in God to feel its efficacy in the experiential world. Most people sensitized to creativity would affirm the spirit as a concrete datum of our psychic life, a constituent element of the human reality. Many sense its inexplicability in scientific categories and are awestruck by its mystery. Some experience the psychological dimension of the spirit so intensely that they are even willing to posit its ontological transcendence as well. For such people, God and the spirit are virtually identical.

The holy, unlike the soul, is not a subjective aspect of religion. Nor is it, like the spirit, that power of the soul which achieves self-transcendence in creative acts. The holy is an oblique way of talking about God. To say that things are holy is tantamount to saying that somehow God is in them. For some, this means that divinity and the substance of the object are one: divinity is immanent in nature; holiness is physical and magical. For others, God is not to be identified with nature itself; rather, God's sovereign power and will invest neutral matter with

161

holiness and significance. Thus, for the Jew, the land and people of Israel are not holy *a priori* but only become so at a moment in history when God, by an act of selection, touches them with His presence, endowing them with the aura of His personhood.

Now if the holy is virtually synonymous with God, why do so many prefer to talk about the experience of the holy, rather than directly affirming the experience of God or the belief in Him? For many, especially those with a sense of delicacy in such matters, the use of the more oblique term preserves the privacy of the experience: one does not talk about God—or love—publicly or too directly. For others, the use of the term *holy* rather than God resolves a serious philosophical problem. While their empiricism prevents them from talking about God as an ontological reality, their experience of certain phenomena and situations is so profoundly "religious" that a word is needed to express its intensity, but it must be a word that will resolve the tension between feeling and thought that such experience occasions. For them, talking about the experience of the holy rather than about the knowledge of God provides such a resolution.

But just how is the holy experienced? For many, it is a quality inherent in certain manifestations of the spirit. At first, the reaction to the holy may be one of attraction, of aesthetic appreciation. Gradually this feeling may turn into one of awe. But it may go beyond this to encompass a moral and personal dimension an well. The holy is associated with that elusive x-factor—intensely experienced but almost incapable of definition—which somehow redeems life from its radical emptiness and, paradoxically, provides something worth dying for. The holy has something ultimate about it: ultimate in the ecstasy one feels when confronted with it, ultimate in the urgency of the demands it places on us. The holy is inviolate and is somehow associated with the self (or the soul). Therefore, he who defiles the holy kills a part of the self. Conversely, he who has a soul knows on some level the immediacy and the coerciveness of the holy.

Thus, loosely speaking, the soul is that sector of the psychic life which senses in certain manifestations of the spirit the quality of holiness. The soul, the spirit, and the holy are considered—rightly or wrongly—as actual categories of man's psychological being. For some, the affirmation that such experiential categories do exist is sufficient. Others, however, seem to need some ontological or metaphysical underpinning for these categories, which they seek in God, the locus—or even creator—of the soul, the spirit, and the holy. Those who are skeptical of the existence of such unverifiable entities might consider the word *God* to be the spirit's noble attempt to explain to itself the source of its own transcendence, to describe a reality in which the soul, the spirit, and the holy are one. Even though this attempt is doomed to failure, it does point out that the workings of the spirit are forever a mystery, even to itself, and that the God who is more than model or metaphor is somehow a part of that very mystery.

THE SPIRIT AND THE PHYSICAL WORLD: A TYPOLOGY OF OTHER RELIGIOUS APPROACHES

With these definitions in hand, a second step to ground our understanding before we turn to the Jewish view is to examine some of the other important types of relation between God and the world that have been typical of other religious traditions. That typology can serve several functions. First, it provides a dramatic foil that can help us highlight what is essential in a Judaic view of the world. Second, we see from the comparison that each of these approaches has its own virtues and limitations. None succeeds entirely, yet each sees a truth not seen by the others.

However, the humbling realization that any attempt to make complete sense of the world is as difficult as attempting to square the circle should not lead us to avoid completely the task of theologizing; neither should we try to escape into either valuationally neutral areas such as abstract mathematics, where the truth of the proposition is its beauty, or more objective fields where factuality is at least an approachable goal.

Whether we acknowledge it or not, all of us try to make some sense of the world; it seems to be our nature to do so. Those who say they don't, do so unconsciously and, more often than not, badly. However, those who consciously philosophize should arm themselves with the foreknowledge that they are engaged in a pursuit that is ultimately tragic, one they cannot win but also cannot abandon. Only God knows all. To make peace with the paradox of a God who gave us enough mind to ask ultimate questions but not enough mind to answer them is to be truly wise and truly human.

A word of caution. The religious types described in the following section are to some degree universal, that is, they are not necessarily limited to any one religion, although most often they find their classical expression in one of the "great" religious traditions. Each religion usually comprises within its historical experience a wide range of types: some reflecting inner polarities, such as Halakhah and Aggadah in Judaism; others reflect outside influences, like that which Greek philosophy and various forms of Gnosticism have had on all three monotheistic religions. It is our awareness of the extraordinary richness and spiritual variety characteristic of almost all the so-called higher religions that prompts us to talk in phenomenological rather than purely historical terms in the following section.

What is presented here is a set of ideal-types that find their most radical crystallization in an important branch of a given religion at a particular period of its development. Suffice it to say that each religion, when studied from the inside in all its historical complexity, may appear to the outsider as many religions. Yet, at the same time, sometimes it is only when an outsider studies a particular religion, with all its varieties and contradictions, that its distinctive characteristics clearly emerge.

164

HUMANISM, ANCIENT AND MODERN

Humanism takes an essentially optimistic attitude toward existence: the world is basically a good place to live in; order, not chaos, prevails; good will exceeds malice. Most of the evils of the world are the products of man's folly or self-indulgence. Most evils, therefore, can be eliminated by the use of common sense and by the application of science to the problems of human existence. Rationality is the hallmark of this approach, and man is considered, rightly or wrongly, a highly educable creature.

This attitude is most attractive to many Jews. Certainly, our tradition has never denied the value of common sense, rationality, or education for the solution of human problems. Nor has Judaism, at least in its biblical manifestation, considered the world to be an essentially bad place in which to live; at least as it emerged from the hands of the Creator, it was "very good" indeed.[2]

These obvious virtues of the humanist view should not blind us to its principal fault: its failure to take into account much of the intractable evil of this world, especially the evil that is not the immediate consequence of man's error and ignorance. This view pays little or no attention to death; to the inability of our intelligence to give meaning to much of life; or to the perversity of men, who, though sensitive in the arts and learned in the sciences, are nevertheless failures as human beings. The slogan "more rationality" simply does not address these phenomena. And above all, the inexplicable nature of existence—if you will, its mysterious quality—is denied. One does not have to be a Freudian to realize that denial is the result of fear: all of us fear death, fear the unknown. Some face this fear; others simply repress it.

THE SPIRITUAL RADICAL

At the opposite pole to the humanists are those, such as Buddhists, who are intensely aware of the imperfection of existence. For them, the very fact of living is a kind of mistake: It is shot through with pain, with the emptiness of fulfilled desire and the frustration of unfulfilled desire, with transience and meaningless repetition, and, above all, with the fallibility of our senses. In fact, all unredeemed men—that is, most of mankind—must suffer the material world and their material, sensate bodies as they would a disease. The enlightened, however, understand that the world of birth and death is but an illusion and that only when human beings learn to see it as such can they achieve blessedness. We suffer evil only because we believe in the reality of our individual and differentiated personalities. As discrete entities, we suffer the anxieties of desire, jealousy, and pain. However, once we overcome the misleading differentiation of persons, of the I and the Thou, and achieve oneness with Being itself, we experience the blessedness of nonbeing, a state free of evil and immune to pain, and also devoid of choice, volition, and responsibility.

In this system, evil is experienced so deeply that, for life to go on, existence itself has to be redefined. One can reject this attitude for its lack of realism, yet one can only be moved by the human ache that motivates it, by its inner calm, and by its attempt to conquer the pain of existence through the application of mind. For the Jew, however, such a system, in its radical denial of reality, is the antithesis of biblical faith.

THE SPIRITUAL REBEL

There are some who, like the spiritual radicals, experience life's evils fully but who, unlike the radicals, refuse to dismiss these evils as illusory. Evil for them is so real that it cannot be dismissed quietly as a disease of perception to be cured by self-enlightenment. This world, in all its concreteness and with all its limitations and imperfections, is so totally perverse, so pervaded by evil, that only a demon or a maniac bent on causing unending suffering for mankind could have conceived of it. The grotesque plan of creating a world so utterly devoid of spirituality, holiness, and goodness, could only have been hatched by a demon. The latter is often identified with the biblical Creator. The God of true spirituality has nothing to do with the world of flesh and form; He is in hiding, and only faint rays of His presence are occasionally felt by the illuminated.

In place of intellectual calm and repose, historically identified with one or another form of Buddhism, this system—usually called Gnosticism—is possessed by an almost Promethean anger, a profound resentment against the cosmic status quo. At times, one is tempted to admit that its description of reality fits the facts better than any other system. It is this seeming correctness that has engendered the Gnostic attitude in all sorts of places and periods: in Persia, in medieval France, and in the very heart of Judaism.

However, if the Gnostic description of reality seems correct, one can only shudder at its prescription. Since the chaos of evil is real and not a delusion, it cannot be transcended by any mental effort; rather, it must be shattered by an eruption of equally chaotic spirituality. If there is a God—and the Gnostics believe that there is—He must be hiding in the realm of pure spirit, unfettered by the limitations of time and space. Man wants to become one with this spirit. Everything connected with our world—law, structure, distinctions of good and evil, rationality, measure, the self in its present form—all of these hold man back and must be eliminated. They constitute a prison that must be shattered to free the soul to return to its source. Only nihilistic and antinomian acts of rebellion against the norms of this world can break open the prison. Matter and the flesh are combated by the Gnostic in two ways: by an extreme asceticism, which kills the self by mortification; and by an extreme orgiastic license, which fights fire with fire, feeding the Devil with his own evil till his belly bursts.[3]

REALITY IS TAINTED, BUT GRACE INTERVENES

Buddhism and Gnosticism face the evil of this worldly existence, and each in its own uncompromising way attempts to transcend it. There are others, mostly Christians, who are unable to accept the simple solution of a demonic world and a transcendent spirit. They face the horrible paradox of a God who created the world in His goodness and a humanity that is corrupt and incapable, by itself, of redemption. It is as if Judaism and Gnosticism were fighting over the soul of Christianity. Like Gnosticism, Christianity is acutely aware of the pain that pervades the world and the weakness and sin that pervade man's nature. Yet, like Judaism, it also affirms the underlying goodness of creation. The solution to this paradox lies in the notion of Satan, an evil power within this world, and of an unmerited salvation wrought by God in a world beyond. If it were not for the benign condescension of a deity who came into this world incarnate to save man from his condition, all would be lost. It is not man's love for God that counts but God's love for man.[4]

Ironically, the Jews, whose history has been marked so much more consistently by suffering than that of the Christians, find it difficult to understand the latter's preoccupation with sin, death, evil, human depravity, and especially the inability of man to achieve his own redemption. Although Jews and Christians share the idea that it is God who takes the initiative in His relations to man, the two faiths part company when it comes to the reasons for this initiative.

For Christians, God condescends to save man from his worthlessness. One can almost say with Marcion: the more worthless the recipient of the divine grace, the more loving the divine donor. For Jews, God enters the world to form a contractual relationship, one could almost say a partnership, with man. The Rabbis, who were no mean students of the Bible, knew of man's sinfulness, but they also knew that they were sons of the King and partners with Him in creating a moral world through the instrumentality of the Law. In one religion, God comes down to save: the greater the depravity of the sinner, the greater the power and mystery of His love. In the other religion, He comes down as a lawgiver and a teacher. His greatest joy is independent students who so master the inner workings of the Law that on occasion they can actually master the teacher at His own game (cf. Babylonian Talmud, *Pesahim* 119a).

For all the reservations Jews have about Christianity—with its otherworldliness, its seeming obsession with sin and salvation, its insufficient recognition of man's creative partnership with God, and of the mind-expanding joy of the study of the Torah—no sensitive person can deny the nobility and bravery of the Christian in trying to balance two conflicting realities, God's goodness and the world's evil. One may be outraged at the central myth of Christianity: the drama of the crucified God. But even the outraged can only marvel at the great religious power of this drama and the unique catharsis it provides for the emotions associated with the great traumas of existence: birth, suffering, and death.

Empirically speaking, the simple fact that some people manage to survive the evils of this world with their humanity intact can only be explained as a gift of divine grace, whether the God who bestows it is incarnate or not. The Jew may not like the term *grace,* but no other word describes the matter more accurately.

Most historical confrontations between the spirit and the physical world—with the notable exception of humanism, both ancient and modern—have seen the world as the enemy of the spirit. Few men have had the calm of the classical Greek religionist, for whom the world was *kosmos,* "eternal order," reflected in the movement of the heavenly bodies along their time-honored paths according to unchanging, immanent laws.

Many have been inclined to see the world quite differently, as a temporary order imposed on an intractable chaos that threatened to break forth at any moment (so ancient Mesopotamian man).

Others went even further. The world—with all of its order, temporary or eternal—is a physical impediment to the achievement of spiritual liberation or religious perfection. It is a burden to be sloughed off, a contamination to be avoided, a deception of the senses to be cured, a plight requiring redemption. This attitude is characteristic of what I have called the radical and rebellious spiritualists—especially the Gnostics—for whom law is in many ways the very symbol of unredeemed reality. It is the inner working of that very nature, both physical and psychological, that he refuses to accept. Through Gnosis, law could be either transcended or broken. For Christianity, at least in some early formulations and in Luther, law is an embarrassing reminder of man's basic sinfulness and of his impotence to overcome sin. Law thus has to be replaced by grace from on high.

NINETEEN

A JEWISH VIEW OF GOD'S RELATION
TO THE WORLD

Judaism, at least in some of its biblical and rabbinic manifestations, stands apart from the models we have just explored. For
the radical spiritualist, such an idea is inconceivable, even impious. How could the divine spirit willfully contaminate itself by
direct contact with the physical world? How could it build into
the world the very laws that would inhibit man's spiritual quest?
For God to seek some sort of fulfillment in the world, to use it
as the stage for the workings of the spirit, seems to the radical
spiritualist the very antithesis of true faith. Yet this is what much
of the Jewish tradition seems to be saying.

THE WORLD AS A NECESSARY GROUND OF ACTION

Let us clarify this point by analogy. A gifted dramatist has finally
put his ideas down on paper. His play—the essence of his dreams
and efforts—lies inert on his desk. The dramatist, unfortunately,
is held captive in the blueprint of his play until live actors realize
his intentions on an actual stage. If he were a painter or a sculp-
tor, his own creative efforts would be sufficient. However, as a

dramatist (or composer) he needs the participation of performers to translate the play (or score) into reality. The performers, however, are also faced with their own problem: how to remain true to their own feelings without being disloyal to the dramatist's intentions. If they simply read their lines without projecting their own feelings, they kill the spirit of the play; if they make up new lines, they subvert its inner form. Everything depends on their balance and delicacy, empathy and control.

The analogy is clear. The Torah is God's play—the blueprint of a moral world waiting to be realized. The physical world, with its water and dry land and necessary imperfections, is the stage on which the drama will unfold. This world—existence, reality, matter—is, in a poetic sense, a divine necessity. It is the raw material in which the creative urge is satisfied and finds form. To deny the world is to deny the God who created it.

The radical spiritualist is appalled by this drama, because it affirms and glorifies all that he most fears and hates; it implies that God, although free from the physical limitations of time and space, magic and coercion, nevertheless acts as if motivated by a spiritual "need": the need to realize a moral order. It implies that He who is most free from the limitations of the world is nevertheless limited in his "dependence" on a human partner, the actual builder of the moral world.

MAN'S PLACE IN THE DIVINE DRAMA

For man to be a partner, he must be free. The inner dialectic of God's plan requires a being armed with intelligence and the ability to make choices, hence also the potential of rebellion and sin. While rebellion destroys creation and the possibility of partnership, an automaton devoid of impulses, like the angels, would lack the capacity to create. Unfortunately, it is this very creative factor that often subverts the plan. According to the Talmud, God was well aware of this difficulty: He was torn between His desire to realize the Torah and His knowledge that man, armed with freedom, could wreak chaos and destroy the world. Nevertheless, in an act of divine "bravery," He created man.

This often tragic tension in the divine mind—between realism and love—is beautifully reflected in the following midrash:

> When God was about to create the world, He said to His angelic council: "Shall we create man in our image?" A group of angels stepped forward and offered this advice: "Lord of the Universe! Consider man's potential for evil: he will lie, murder, commit adultery, and create weapons to destroy Your world. Don't go through with the plan." However, the divine urge to create a human partner was so great that no argument, however realistic, was tolerated. The Lord stretched forth His little finger, let loose a surge of energy, and burned the angels, the heavenly realists, to a crisp. Other groups made similar suggestions and were treated in a similar fashion, until the angels acquiesced to the divine desire and gave their approval, saying: "Lord, the world is Yours. Do with it as You see fit."[1]

The predictions of the angels came true in full measure. Adam was given one commandment and broke it. Eve was tempted by the serpent. Cain murdered his brother, and his not-so-distant relative made weapons of iron to kill more men. All of this, together with the general corruption of man, brought on the Flood. But even after this chastisement, Noah, the man who was "just in his generation" had nothing better to do after escaping the wrath of the waters than to drown himself in wine. Then came the Tower of Babel, after which, according to the midrash, the angels came before God and said, in a tone of not-so-gentle admonition: "The first group of angels were not so wrong after all."

The Rabbis of the midrash realized that without human freedom and all that it implies—instinctual urges and the capacity to destroy as well as to create—the law would be irrelevant.[2] When the angels suggested that the Torah be given to them instead of to man, God replied: "Do you lie, do you steal, do you have an evil inclination?" Without man, the law is irrelevant; without freedom and instinct, man is not human.

It is related that after the Men of the Great Assembly had arranged for the *yeṣer haraʿ* (evil inclination) of idolatry to be eliminated, they decided to get rid of its partner, the overall *yeṣer*, the source of all instinct. They offered a petition to the divine court and their request was granted. The *yeṣer* was incarcerated; no longer would it stimulate the world. However, three days later someone went out to look for a fresh egg to cure a sick person, and, lo and behold, there were no fresh eggs to be found. The generative processes had come to a halt. Because the *yeṣer* was inactive, chickens were not laying eggs, and the work of creation had begun to founder. The Men of the Great Assembly were faced with a grave problem: to let the *yeṣer* loose was to court danger; to fetter it completely was to destroy the world. They came to the following solution: let it loose, but put a pair of blinders on its eyes; regulate its excitations, but do not get rid of them.[3]

The *yeṣer* is the yeast of creation. It makes bread rise and stimulates human beings to struggle constructively in a process known as *yishuvo shel ʿolam* (the settling of the world). Like some vital nutriments before adequate preparation, the *yeṣer haraʿ* in its raw state is dangerous and destructive.[4] However, when processed by the Torah and sublimated by the rationality of the law, it becomes a vital, constructive element in human life. As energy in the raw, it destroys; structured and channeled, it creates.

Law is not merely God's dream, the plan of a new world, but also the instrument that humanizes man sufficiently to participate in the fulfillment of this plan. Man is created in the divine image; but as image, his is an unrealized potential. Only by becoming human under the guidance of the law does man actualize this potential.

THE LAW, DEATH, AND KNOWLEDGE

Law is in its essence a limit and a boundary. Our biological being is subject to the law of death; our intellectual grasp is limited by the law of the senses. Religions of radical spirituality rebel against these limits and, in their hubris, create intellectual Towers of Babel to storm the heights of the spirit. Through Gnosis, knowledge, or enlightenment, man imagines he can transcend his biological finiteness, become one with the infinite and eternal spirit, and achieve immortality—in short, become like the gods.

Judaism is not a religion of radical spirituality but one of law and limitation. God created the world with these bounds in mind, and man must humbly make his peace with them. For man to believe that through knowledge he can transcend the limits of life and become eternal is to deny that God is truly the Lord. The Midrash states this insight with typical poetic breadth: "God anticipated that Nebuchadnezzar and Hiram, king of Tyre, would some day, in their hubris, declare that they were divine. Therefore, as a preventive measure, He decreed death for Adam and for all mankind."[5] Death, according to monotheism, is the built-in protection against man's latent tendency to proclaim his own divinity.

In cultures where man thought he could become like a god and live forever, knowledge—either in the form of a secret or a philosophical discipline—was often considered the key to eternal life. The Sumerican hero Gilgamesh seeks out Utnapishtim, survivor of the great Flood, for this reason; and men joined mystery religions—all in search of knowledge that made men like gods, immortal.[6] However, in Israel, where the gap between man and God was absolute, nothing, not even knowledge, could bring about such a transformation. As long as biblical man accepted the authority of God, he was forced to make peace with his mortality and use his mind, not for the purpose of becoming like God, but simply to grasp and apply His commands to live justly in an imperfect world.

THE HUMANITY OF GOD

The ultimate principles of most religions are the stumbling blocks of their believers. This is especially true of the faiths of radical spirituality. All religions set as their ultimate goal the imitation of the Divine. Yet a God who is presented in terms of absolute perfection, noninvolvement, self-sufficiency, and omniscience is not a viable model for human behavior. Such a model is a stumbling block for most human beings, one way or another. The spiritual aristocrats will say, in their arrogance, "If the Divine is perfect, all-knowing, and above the fetters and limitations of reality, I will attain the same attributes; I too can achieve liberation from reality." These holy spirits, however, usually collapse in their attempt to transcend their creatureliness, the limits inherent in their bodies and souls. The rest of humanity will find such an ideal totally unrealistic and will not even attempt an approximation. In fact, the radical perfection of the image may only discourage them and lead them into greater inhumanity.

The Rabbis, in their wisdom, tell us of the sins of the saints. In this they follow the Bible.[7] They even add sins that the Bible does not tell us about. All of this is done with the intuitive genius of the master pedagogue. An educational model has to lend itself to imitation. One cannot imitate perfection, and there is little personal empathy between the sinner and the perfect saint. But if David, the great and noble king, sinned and yet was able to repent, every man is capable of empathizing with him and thus imitating him. David is noble even though flawed, and that is why he can serve as a model.

This principle can be extended mythically—that is, seriously but not literally—to the Divine. God in His infinite wisdom knew that if He revealed His true, transcendent nature to man, He would cause great havoc. Therefore, He donned a human persona. He appeared before man as a personality: exalted, yet fallible and warm. He entered into a contractual relationship with man, became involved in the human condition, experienced exasperation over the hardness of men's hearts, regretted that He had ever created man, was moved by the intercession of Moses and other prophets, broke out into fits of rage over the sinfulness of His people, and was so involved with Israel that despite their sinfulness He actually re-espoused them after having delivered them the bill of divorcement. God appears to experience all the human emotions: love, anger, involvement, indignation, regret, sadness, and so on. By so doing, He gives the seal of divinity to the very essence of our humanity. He implicitly says to man: "You cannot know what is above and what is below, but you can know what is in your hearts and in the world. These feelings and reactions and emotions that make up human existence are, if illumined by faith and rationality, all the divinity you can hope for. To be humane is to be divine: as I am holy, so you shall be holy; as I am merciful, so you shall be merciful." Thus, there is only one kind of knowledge that is open to man, the knowledge of God's humanity:

> Let not the wise man boast of his wisdom,
> Nor let the strong man boast of his strength,
> Nor the rich man boast of his riches!
> Rather it is in this that a man should take pride:
> That he knows and attends Me,
> That I, YHWH, am He who practices kindness,
> Justice, and righteousness on Earth;
> For in these things I delight. (Jer. 9:22–23)

Neither the secrets of the universe nor the Gnosis that transcends death, but obedience to those human attributes in which God, in His divine wisdom, clothes Himself to serve as the model of human behavior—this is the deeper meaning of the statement that "the Torah speaks in human language."

The purpose of much of the Aggadah is to humanize the image of God and, in so doing, to humanize men created in this image. I end this discussion with a midrash:[8]

> How does God spend his time? During the first third of the day, as divine judge and cosmic administrator He recites this prayer: "May it be My will that My love for humanity overcome My exasperation with them!" During the second third of the day, He takes out the Torah and studies. And during the third part of the day, He is the cosmic matchmaker who brings man and wife together.[9]

Here is the quintessence of humanity and spiritual realism. It is as if to say that God has a devotional life, an intellectual life, and a life of loving social responsibility; these are the really divine traits. He is the administrator of the world, and as such, He faces all the problems that the human power-holder faces. If He did not love human beings, He would put an end to them; yet they are exasperating, so He prays that He has the strength to stand this inner tension. In making marriages he joins the intimate life of his creations, expressing love that we, too, experience. He is also constantly studying, so that if you imagine you "know it all," consider God and see that even He, at least poetically speaking, does not. Therefore, study!

Twenty

JUDAISM AND SECULAR CULTURE

AN HISTORICAL DIALECTIC

The relationship between Judaism and the surrounding non-Jewish culture has always been a dialectical one. The pattern was set early on by the tension between biblical monotheism and paganism. On the one hand, the pagan world was in the one in which monotheism had been born, the world of which, to this extent, it was a part. On the other hand, it was the world with which monotheism fought; hence it was the "enemy." Finally, it was the world monotheism helped to reshape by contributing to it from its own unique fund of ideas.

No matter how unique the idea of biblical monotheism may have been, how inexplicable in terms of preceding religious developments, the actual forms in which the idea became a historical reality—law, cult, kingship, prophecy, and so forth—all have clear Near Eastern antecedents. Furthermore, this dependence is more than a receptivity to forms. The very ethos of the Bible, its relative sophistication, and especially its highly developed legal structure and concern for social justice—all bear an unmistakably Mesopotamian stamp. Yet, in spite of the Bible's debt to Mesopotamia, it was against this very environment that monotheism was to declare an uncompromising war, one which was to affect the very shape of Western culture.

In subsequent periods of Jewish history this dialectic of receptivity, rejection, and influence carried over into Judaism's relation to secular culture. Thus, without the threat and stimulus of the Hellenistic experience, postexilic Judaism might never have recovered from its century-long slumber, might never have produced the religious culture reflected in the Talmud and Midrash, or the speculations of its mystics or the history-making activities of its sectarians. Yet instead of succumbing to the Greek presence, as did so many other peoples (with the notable exception of the Romans), the Jews creatively assimilated the Greek culture into their own, illumining their own law with its dialectic, stimulating their literature—the Aggadah—with its aesthetic, and ultimately creating a new synthesis that not only influenced the Greek world, in turn, but also helped to bring about its very collapse.

The experience of the Middle Ages is no less instructive. The Greek-Arabic philosophical, scientific, and literary synthesis produced a secular culture that complemented—though it sometimes conflicted with—the religious culture Jews had received from the past. Enamored of this wider culture and illumined by its canons, Judaism now lost some of its old intransigence; even in its own eyes, it was no longer the only source of truth. By the same token, secular culture gave faith the sophistication that came with self-reflection, for it now felt the need to explain itself to itself, in secular terms.

Not everyone, however, saw in secular culture the necessary complement of religion, that which purified religion of its naiveté and curbed some of its excesses. For some, secular culture was simply more real than religion. For others, this culture represented the threat of moral and intellectual nihilism. But even those who felt threatened by it could not escape its power and charm. Indeed their very attacks against secular culture were informed by its logic and influenced by its style. What secular culture did not and could not do was to add significantly to the basic ideas and structures of religion.

INTELLECT AND AESTHETICS

It must be remembered that the impact of secular culture on the Jewish tradition was as subtle and unconscious as it was profound. Few of those influenced were actually aware of the process and, if they had been, many would have resisted it. Many, but not all. In every generation there have been a few religious thinkers, quite aware of the influence of secular culture, who did not necessarily condemn it. The Torah was certainly their primary concern, but the surrounding culture did have its legitimate function in their life. Thus, the exercise of the intellect and even the cultivation of the aesthetic sensibility were seen as having a place, however ancillary, within the divine economy.

These premodern religious evaluations of the secular are not merely of historical interest. For the modern thinker, increasingly concerned with the role of the secular in religious life, these traditional evaluations provide precious guidelines for a modern Judaic theology of culture. In the following section, therefore, we will concern ourselves with the conscious attitudes of tradition to secular culture, specifically to the cultivation of the intellectual and aesthetic dimensions of life, usually the hallmark of the cultivated person.

Unfortunately, traditional sources, especially the more ancient ones, are rarely as self-reflective or articulate in these matters as modern theologians would like. Nevertheless, the sources are not silent. A traditional consensus concerning the uses of the mind would be something like this: any intellectual skill or discipline is to be valued if (a) it is not inherently associated with paganism, (b) it is not cultivated as an end in itself, and (c) it is directed to the constructive solution of practical problems.

Although revelation (Torah) is a superior form of knowledge, secular wisdom *(ḥokhmah)*, too, is to be considered one of God's blessings to man, not merely Jewish man.

This attitude is evident in many statements of the Rabbis and implicit in many biblical passages. Thus, although men of *ḥokhmah* like Solomon (who knew the languages of the animals) and Bezalel (who had the skill to build the Tabernacle) were not numbered among the saints, they did merit a place among traditional culture-heroes. The *B'nei Kedem* (Moabites, Edomites, Ammonites, etc.) are praised for their *ḥokhmah* in the poetic arts, and some of their compositions are even quoted in the Pentateuch (cf. Num. 21:27). The Bible even seems to have a grudging respect for the efficacy of pagan magic and sooth-saying, though it forbids their use as idolatrous.

But when not idolatrous, *ḥokhmah*, whatever its source, is welcomed. Thus, Greek techniques used in editing the classics are creatively applied by the Rabbis to the editing of the Bible; Greek science and medicine are used to solve halakhic problems; Greek rhetoric is used to sharpen the minds of rabbinic legalists. Even a rapid perusal of Lieberman's classic books *Greek in Jewish Palestine* and *Hellenism in Jewish Palestine* gives the impression that the incorporation of Greek methods was not merely an un-conscious sociological trend but a process the Rabbis consciously fostered.[1]

Finally, it should be noted that the Rabbis were aware that much of their law, especially law related to documents, had an external Near Eastern source. The expression *leshon hedyot* (layman's formulary), used by the Talmud to describe rabbinic legal documents, reflects the Rabbis' awareness that the law of documents was of non-Jewish, or at least non-rabbinic, origin. What was uniquely Jewish was not the law itself—this was more or less common to all Mesopotamians, Jews and Gentiles alike—but rather the passionate concern to see God's demands for jus-tice realized. If the *ḥokhmah* of non-Jewish law proved useful for this purpose, it too could be assimilated.

The Middle Ages are no exception to this trend. Arabic medicine and science were avidly pursued even by the most traditional. Jewish doctors and scientists were well known throughout the medieval world. Maimonides, the great master of Jewish law, was also the physician to the sultan's court and the author of scientific treatises on rock science and botany. The fact that many popes had Jewish doctors is well known. In our time, the affinity between Orthodox Jews and the sciences, especially physics, mathematics, and medicine, is also well known and not a mere coincidence. To sum up: The application of the mind to the solution of practical and technical problems has always been looked on favorably by the tradition if these activities do not distract the man of faith from the central concerns of life: the study of the Torah and the observance of the commandments.

QUESTIONING GOD

As long as human intelligence is applied to useful human purposes, it poses little threat to religion. However, once the mind starts to search for understanding—of its own workings, of nature, and especially of God—it confronts faith with a powerful adversary. The speculative intelligence questions everything; nothing escapes its probing. Is the God who exists a real force in the world? If so, is He a force for good? The question may be irrelevant: He may not exist at all.

Questions about God are not necessarily the enemy of theistic religion. They are dangerous only if faith is defined as the transcending of rationality, the belief in something beyond the boundaries of logic, "the absurd." According to this Kierkegaardian approach, typical of some types of Christianity and of certain trends in the Bible (cf. the ʿAqedah story in Gen. 22), faith and doubt are in polar opposition. However, there is another type of faith represented in the Bible, one more "empirical" and almost tolerant of the frame of mind that insists that "seeing is believing."

Instead of demanding affirmations of the mind that are rationally absurd, it calls for loyalty to the God who has manifested His power in the past and for a sense of trust in His power to deliver in the future. The only "heresy" the Bible knows is disloyalty to God after having experienced His goodness (cf. Deut. 1:32ff. and Jer. 2:5ff., among others).

Furthermore, the biblical God even allows Himself to be tested. Instead of being offended by Gideon's doubts that He was really speaking to him, God actually goes along with Gideon's desire to authenticate the vision by a sign—in effect, to subject Him to a scientific experiment. Gideon even has the audacity to request a second "experiment," a "control," lest the first sign merely be a coincidence! The extent to which God tolerates this skeptical frame of mind and the empirical methods by which He overcomes Gideon's doubts are truly remarkable (cf. Judg. 6). At least in one case in the Bible, it is not the testing of God that arouses divine ire, but the refusal to test Him: King Ahaz declines to test God's power when a choice of authenticating experiments ("signs") is offered the king by the prophet (cf. Isa. 7:10ff.).

God does not want to outrage the human mind by demanding affirmations of faith not grounded in experience. Furthermore, when experience conflicts with preconceived notions about divine justice, biblical religion does not seem to require the man of faith to repress his doubts in silent resignation. Abraham, Jeremiah, and Job, all men who question God's ways, are hardly numbered among the wicked. There is even some evidence that God demands such criticism, at least from His prophets (cf. Ezek. 22:30).

However, the doubt tolerated by the Bible is radically different from that generated by philosophical speculation. Job's mind may doubt God's justice, but his heart never for a moment doubts God's existence. It is just this discrepancy that produces Job's anguish; to feel that God exists, yet to know that He is unjust, is more than the mind can bear. In contrast, a capricious or even wicked god is not a problem for the Job character in the parallel Babylonian version of the story, because he never assumes that the gods are, or have to be, just.

Philosophical doubt is something entirely different. Philosophy has the power to declare religious feelings meaningless and to deny not only God's justice, but His existence as well. Such radical doubt is something that few religions or, for that matter, political systems are prepared to accept without reservation. For theistic religion to allow room for atheism is to court suicide. Yet, religious and political establishments realize, usually after bitter experience, that it is much wiser to contain free thinkers by allowing them carefully circumscribed areas of freedom than to repress them altogether and thus unwittingly bring about an explosion of real heresy, a threat to the stability of church and state alike. This is the best any polity can do for its intellectuals.

Realistically speaking, no belief system can leave room for a free questioning of its own first principles. It is doubtful whether even democracy can allow those living under its aegis the right to question freely the validity of the democratic process. And yet, as long as those who have their doubts do not actively advocate the overthrow of the legal framework of democracy, the doubters are still allowed to voice their opinions. On occasion, these opinions may even help democracy to realize itself more fully. The question facing us is, To what degree do the study of history, psychology, and philosophy—and the doubts they create in our minds—actually contribute to the deepening of our religious life?

In most cases, their contribution is not very constructive. On the surface, the probing of the historian into the genesis of religion and the investigations of the psychologists into the nature of the psyche are rarely conducive to greater religiosity. A rigid historian tends to explain everything in terms of concrete, immanent causes, leaving little room for transcendental influences, much less divine intervention in the course of events. There is also little room for God alongside the id, ego, and superego.

Yet, the honest religionist can no more deny his religious feelings than he can the logic of science. Both make absolute claims on his loyalty. Instead of resolving this tension by eliminating one of the discordant poles, he bravely holds both poles simultaneously, having learned to live with this tension as a constituent element in his life. This dialectic is similar to that of the checks and balances built into political systems: no one branch of the government exercises absolute power. Similarly, no one mode of observation, be it history, religion, sociology, or aesthetics, can comprehend all of reality. Each of them, to be sure, makes absolute, hence idolatrous claims that it alone holds the key to the truth. But by setting the various modes of observation in dialectical tension with each other, the excessive claims of each mode are checked, their idolatrous tendencies are restrained, and a modicum of balance may be achieved. Thus, for example, science challenges the myths of religion, but religion, in turn, challenges the moral nihilism of science.

The same holds true concerning the dialogue between religions. By comparing one religion with another, not only are the implicit assumptions of one's own faith made clearer, but the inherent tendency of every faith to make itself the measure of all things is checked. Historically speaking, religions are always aware of their limitations; otherwise, they would not borrow so freely from one another. These borrowings do not signal the death of a religion but its spiritual health, its realization that the truth it needs but does not possess can be borrowed from the outside and assimilated into its own creative genius.

The doubt stimulated by critical inquiry is healthy for yet another reason: it tests our faith and separates the person of real faith from the religious behaviorist. Faith is not a passive state, a status quo, but an inner struggle. It is an order superimposed on a chaos that constantly threatens to break forth. It is doubt that stirs inert hearts from their complacency and sets the dialectic of faith and doubt in motion. Furthermore, the greater the faith, the greater the amount of doubt the man of faith will be able to digest without losing his equilibrium. If the man of faith has the good fortune to come out of this battle without having denied either religion or science, he will unknowingly have developed a new skill: the ability to hold life like a bird, tightly enough that it doesn't fly away, gently enough that it isn't choked to death.

TWENTY-ONE

ON THE DEMYTHOLOGIZING

OF RELIGION

DEWEY AND THE NEW THEOLOGIANS

Reading John Dewey's 1934 book *A Common Faith,* I was struck by the extent to which the New Theology of the mid-twentieth century seems like a page out of his thought.[1] This is especially true of the New Theology's *ressentiment* against the supernatural God of traditional religion, rightly or wrongly considered an obstacle to man's spiritual maturity and a stumbling block in the way of his engagement with the problems of the real world. But while the common, demythologized faith of Dewey and the New Theologians appears (to both positivists and theists alike) as nothing but a slightly disguised atheism, both still speak of "the religious" as a real and positive component of human experience.

The difference between Dewey and the latter-day demythologizers is often a matter of style rather than substance. While Dewey made the transition from traditional religion to humanistic faith with philosophical cool, the New Theologians seem to take an emotional delight in slaying God the Father in order to assert their own selfhood. While both are optimistic about the human situation, the New Theologians are often possessed by an eschatological enthusiasm, which may be an expression of relief upon being "liberated" from a Christian or existentialist pessimism or even from a Niebuhrian realism.

The substantial identity of much of Dewey's "common faith" with the New Theology, especially his rejection of a supernatural God, leads one to suspect that if Dewey were read more by contemporary theological audiences, he would not seem like a stranger to them. They might even be a bit stunned to realize that styles operate in theology as well as in clothes and that old men well trained in philosophy are often more profound than young men who make the pages of *Time*. As for me, my reading of *A Common Faith* forced me to admit that the closely parallel Kaplanian Reconstructionism of my teens, which I had left for the profounder thought of Heschel, Niebuhr, and Tillich, had made a deeper impression on me than I had realized.

Intellectual commonplaces, and much of Dewey on religion seems to me to be just that, frequently need to be restated and reexperienced. In this case, such a restatement can be healthiest for those who have come to a Heschelian position embracing a supernatural God without having gone through the agony of a humanistic demythologization of religion, such as Dewey so effectively provides. Thus, for example, there can be no doubt that much of what we say about God is a projection, if not of generalized human ideals, as Dewey would have it, then of an idealized *anthropos,* the best vision of God humanly possible, as Feuerbach viewed it. Furthermore, I have no doubt that supernaturalism and the hypostatizing of human ideals into an all-powerful person who somehow stands above and beyond the world have created a great deal of intellectual mischief. I would agree with Dewey that religion has often sapped man's energies from creative social action and misdirected them into an anti-worldly hostility.

On the positive side, I would also agree with Dewey, as against the more militant atheists, that even if one wishes to avoid speaking about God or religion, it is still legitimate and even necessary to talk about the religious elements of experience. The latter do have an objective reality, no matter how we explain them metaphysically. Furthermore, following Dewey, there can be little doubt that religion has both a psychological and a poetic component. Moments of heightened self-awareness and oneness with the world do have a "religious" quality about them. States of creative tension between ideals imaginatively projected and the here-and-now of the world, states of mind in which one's humanity is explosively expanded, are not unrelated to that reality symbolized by the word *God*.

A POSTSCRIPT FOR DEWEY

It is clear that I do not want to return to what Dewey calls supernaturalism. On the other hand, if one is to remain, at least for the sake of the intellectual game, in his humanistic camp, there are some aspects of his theology that have to be corrected as misrepresentations of how traditional religion actually operates, and there are other aspects of his thought that must be modified in order to strengthen their practical, world-building power, in keeping with Dewey's activist orientation.

The major misrepresentation in Dewey's system is his description of the supernatural God of traditional religion. According to Dewey, the supernatural God is necessarily (a) anti-worldly, (b) a stumbling block to human maturation, and (c) the reflection of a lack of real faith in the self-realizing power of man's own ideals. Historically and phenomenologically, these are distortions. The biblical God, although supernatural—a better word might be "transcendent"—is deeply involved in the world. In fact, paradoxical as it may seem, it is this very transcendence that gives Him the psychological power and the necessary freedom to become personally involved in the human condition. Historically speaking, Western man became human

191

to the degree that this anthropological projection onto the screen of divinity became operative in his own life; man, like God, is free from nature but creatively and lovingly involved in it. One has every right to reject a transcendent God as a philosophical impossibility, but one should be more exact in phenomenological description and historical interpretation.

The religiously oriented humanist may follow Dewey in his rejection of the anthropomorphic God as an ontological reality, but however correct Dewey's revised conception of the deity may be on the philosophical level, it may also be humanly irrelevant. Dewey's God, the totally abstract and highly intellectualized projection of our ideals and aspirations, is utterly lacking in psychological depth and poetic power. This should be seen as regrettable even from Dewey's own point of view, for he himself often stresses the self-unifying psychological value of the religious (if not of God Himself), is deeply aware of the structural similarity between the religious and the poetic, and desperately wants his common faith to have the practical, generative power that only the poetic imagery of religion is capable of inspiring.

A CALL FOR REMYTHOLOGIZING THEOLOGY

It is almost tragic that in order to liberate the religious from religion, the God of the common faith from the God of supernaturalism, it should be necessary to demythologize religious literature, thus draining off its poetic power, and to depersonalize religious doctrine, thus draining it of its educational power. A model of divinity that does not partake of personhood can hardly be expected to cultivate personhood in man. Furthermore, a boring and unevocative model, no matter how correct philosophically, is certainly of little "world-creating" value. The problem, therefore, of the modern religious humanist is how to demythologize the model without sapping its poetic force and psychological profundity.

I believe that many of these pitfalls could be avoided if we remythologized our theology rather than demythologized it. Fully realizing that the anthropomorphic God is to a very great degree a projection of man's understanding of his own psyche (not merely of his own intellectualized and abstracted ideals), we must turn up the mythical decibels of the old personal God. In doing so, we can (a) spell out more clearly the anthropological and psychological implications of the anthropomorphic God and find out exactly what new definitions of personality were being projected by ancient Hebrew man; (b) win the loyalty of the reader of the myth to its humanistic content, not only by the inner cogency of its message, but also by the poetic power of its form; and (c) convince the philosophically oriented reader, by the exaggerated nature of the poetic presentation, that the theologian is as much a demythologizer in his remythologizing as the philosopher is in his abstractions. The sophisticated philosopher, instead of being embarrassed by the personhood and mythic character of the old God, can delight in them as poetically formulated models of man's humanity. He may even ponder for a moment whether or not the power that operates in man to create such humanizing images may not somehow be associated, in fact, with what we usually call God. If the divine projections are not quite ontology, they may be more than mere poetry.

A psychologically oriented, mythically formulated phenomenology of the world-affirming God as He appears in the Bible and in later rabbinic tradition would be valuable to those theists, athesists, and agnostics who cultivate humanistic values. Since the phenomenology can be accepted either as a psychological poem or as a reflection of some ontological reality, it may possibly serve as the basis of a faith which humanists of all kinds can hold in common.

NOTES

Introduction: Monotheism, Anthropomorphism, and the Personhood of God

1. Cf. Yehezkel Kaufmann, *Toledot Ha-'Emunah Ha-Yisra'elit,* 2nd ed., 4 vols. (Jerusalem and Tel Aviv: Bialik and Dvir, 1955–56), 1(II):221–54; Max Kadushin, *The Rabbinic Mind,* 2nd ed. (New York: Blaisdell, 1965), esp. 273ff.; and Gershom Scholem, *Major Trends in Jewish Mysticism,* 3rd ed. (New York: Schocken Books, 1954), esp. 63–67.

Chapter 1: Paganism and Biblical Religion

1. John Bright, *A History of Israel,* 3rd ed. (Philadelphia: Westminster, 1981), 67–103; Cyrus H. Gordon, "Biblical Customs and the Nuzu Tablets," *Biblical Archaeologist Reader* 2 (1964): 21–33.
2. See E. A. Speiser's discussion of Abraham in his *Genesis* (Garden City, N.Y.: Doubleday, 1964).
3. Samuel Noah Kramer, *History Begins at Sumer* (Garden City, N.Y.: Doubleday, 1959), 131.
4. Thorkild Jacobsen, *The Intellectual Adventure of Ancient Man: An Essay on Speculative Thought in the Ancient Near East,* eds. Henri Frankfort et al. (Chicago: University of Chicago Press, 1946), 137ff.
5. Yehezkel Kaufmann, *The Religion of Israel, from Its Beginnings to the Babylonian Exile,* trans. and abr. Moshe Greenberg (Chicago: University of Chicago Press, 1960), 21–59.
6. Ibid., 60–121.

7. Abraham Malamat, "Prophecy in the Mari Documents," *Eretz-Israel* 4 (1956): 74–84; Malamat, "History and a Prophetic Vision in a Mari Letter," *Eretz-Israel* 5 (1958): 67–73.

8. According to Kaufmann (*The Religion of Israel,* 91ff.), the *urim* and *tumim,* a seeming exception to this principle, were of extreme simplicity, almost prescientific. Notice how different this is from the complicated and learned science of the Babylonians. Compared to the prophetic conversations between Moses and God, the *urim* and *tumim* of Aaron are peripheral at most. Furthermore, after the days of David, this mode of consulting the deity almost disappears.

9. Daniel is a second example of an Israelite who interprets omens in the courts of Gentile kings.

Chapter 2: The Essence of the Biblical Process

1. The last paragraph is simply a distillation of Cornford's analysis of Greek religion; see Francis M. Cornford, *From Religion to Philosophy: A Study in the Origins of Western Speculation* (London: Edwin Arnold, 1912). It is identical with Kaufmann's analysis of paganism; see Kaufmann, *The Religion of Israel,* 21ff. Indeed, one who has read Cornford and accepted his interpretation of the Greek religious and intellectual experience and then confronted the Bible with his criteria must arrive independently at the essential position of Kaufmann. What is so interesting is that Kaufmann never mentions Cornford once. The very word *meta-divine,* used by Kaufmann, is also used by Zeller in his discussion of the religion of the Jains, who, like their Middle Eastern counterparts, devalued the realm of the gods. Kaufmann's concept that the term *meta-divine* must, in fact, play a central role in any intelligent investigation of nonbiblical religions is correct.

2. Kaufmann's great contribution is to have approached the Bible from the vantage point of philosophical and mystical paganism, instead of from the point of view of the Bible itself. It is significant that in a certain esoteric tradition, Mesopotamian gods are identified with numbers: Ishtar = 15, Marduk = 40. But this observation must be more thoroughly digested. Saying that a god "is 15" does not mean he is fifteen different entities; rather, that is his code number! See Simo Parpola, "The Assyrian Tree of Life: Tracing the Origins of Jewish Monotheism and Greek Philosophy," *Journal of Near Eastern Studies* 52 (1993): 161–208.

3. This idea is beautifully illustrated by Moshe Maisels in his book *Mahshavah ve-'Emet,* 2 vols. (Tel Aviv: Mitzpeh, 1938–39), under the name M. 'Amishai.

4. Cf. the national psalms, such as Psalms 44 and 60, and the protestations of a Habakkuk, a Job, or a Jeremiah.

5. Walter Eichrodt, *Man in the Old Testament,* trans. K. and R.

Gregor Smith (Chicago: Henry Regnery, 1951), 10.

6. Cf. Hans G. Güterbock, "Die historische Tradition und ihre literarische Gestaltung bei Babyloniern und Hethitern," *Zeitschrift für Assyriologie* 42 (1934): 1–91; Güterbock, "Authority and Law in the Hittite Kingdom," *Supplement to the Journal of American Oriental Society* 10 (1954): 16–24.

Chapter 4: The Gods and the Law

1. Cf. *Enuma Elish;* see E. A. Speiser, trans., "The Creation Epic," in *Ancient Near Eastern Texts Relating to the Old Testament* [*ANET*], 3rd ed., ed. James B. Prichard (Princeton: Princeton University Press, 1969), 60–72.

2. Cf. the red charm Marduk carries in his lips in *Enuma Elish.*

3. Cf. the request of the gods at the end of *Enuma Elish* that Marduk create man to be the valet of the gods; cf. also the Gilgamesh epic: "And the gods gathered around the offerer of the sacrifice like hungry flies."

4. Kramer, *History Begins at Sumer,* 131.

5. This observation is amply confirmed by A. Leo Oppenheim, "The Care and Feeding of the Gods," in his *Ancient Mesopotamia: Portrait of a Dead Civilization* (Chicago: University of Chicago Press, 1964), 183ff.

6. Cf. for example, the cultic content of the "prophetic" condemnation at Mari in Abraham Malamat, "Prophecy in the Mari Documents," *Eretz-Israel* 4 (1956): 74–84; Malamat, "History and a Prophetic Vision in a Mari Letter," *Eretz-Israel* 5 (1958): 67–73.

7. Jacob J. Finkelstein, "Bible and Babel," *Commentary* 26 (1958): 431–44; see also his article, "The West, the Bible and the Ancient Near East: Apperceptions and Categorisations," *Man* 9 (1974): 591–608, also found with slight modification in his "The Ox That Gored," *Transactions of the American Philosophical Society* 71.2 (1981): 1–89 (see pages 7–14 under the section "Appreciations and Categorizations").

8. Robert H. Pfeiffer, trans., "I Will Praise the Lord of Wisdom," in *ANET,* 435.

9. Kaufmann, *Toledot,* 3(II): 79ff.

10. Cf. Thorkild Jacobsen, "Formative Tendencies in Sumerian Religion," in *The Bible and the Ancient Near East: Essays in Honor of William Foxwell Albright,* ed. G. Ernest Wright (Garden City, N.Y.: Doubleday, 1961), 267–78; Benno Landsberger, "Die babylonischen termini für Gesetz und Recht," in *Symbolae ad iura orientis antiqui pertinentes Paulo Koschaker dedicatae,* ed. J. Friedrich et al. (Studia et documenta ad iura orientis antiqui pertinenta 2; Leiden: Brill, 1939), 219–34; Teilhard de Chardin, *The Phenomenon of Man* (New York: Harper, 1959); and Maisels, *Mahshavah ve-'Emet.*

11. Cf. Thorkild Jacobsen, "Mesopotamian Gods and Pantheons," in *Toward the Image of Tammuz and Other Essays on Mesopotamian History and Culture,* ed. William L. Moran (Cambridge, Mass.: Harvard University Press, 1970), 16ff.; Jacobsen, *The Treasures of Darkness: A History of Mesopotamian Religion* (New Haven: Yale University Press, 1976), 6–11.

12. See the discussion of genius in Arthur Koestler's *The Act of Creation* (New York: Macmillan, 1964); and Kaufmann, in his introduction to *Toledot,* 1(I):xxi–xliiii.

13. For these terms, see Moshe Greenberg, "Some Postulates of Biblical Law," in *Yehezkel Kaufmann Jubilee Volume,* ed. Menahem Haran (Jerusalem: Magnes, 1960), 9ff.

14. Finkelstein, "Bible and Babel," *Commentary* 26 (1958): 440ff.

15. Cf. Yehezkel Kaufmann, *The Religion of Israel,* 216ff.

16. Cf. his article "'People' and 'Nation' of Israel," *Journal of Biblical Literature* 79 (1960): 157–63.

17. This interpretation is in harmony with Kaufmann's historical reconstruction as well as Noth's theory concerning the amphyctionic origins of the Jewish people. Cf. Kaufmann, *Toledot* 2(I): 69ff.
    On the comparative studies of law in biblical and Mesopotamian religions, consider also Moshe Greenberg's important article, "Some Postulates of Biblical Criminal Law," in *Yehezkel Kaufmann Jubilee Volume,* ed. M. Haran (Jerusalem: Magnes, 1960), 5–28.

Chapter 6: Biblical Anthropomorphism

1. For the transcendent nature of the biblical God, see Yehezkel Kaufmann, *The Religion of Israel;* but see also Jon D. Levenson, *Creation and the Persistence of Evil: The Jewish Drama of Divine Omnipotence* (San Francisco: Harper & Row, 1988), 3–13.

2. See, for example, Isaak (Yitzhak) Heinemann, "The Struggle against Anthropomorphism in Greece and in Israel," *Iyyun* (1946): 147–65 [in Hebrew]; Kaufmann, *Toledot,* 1(II): 221–54, esp. 238–44. For a general overview of anthropomorphism in Judaism, see Louis Ginzberg, "Anthropomorphism," *The Jewish Encyclopedia,* ed. Isidore Singer, 12 vols. (New York: Funk & Wagnalls Company, 1925), 1:621–25; on anthropomorphism in rabbinic midrash, see David Stern, "*Imitatio Hominis:* Anthropomorphism and Character(s) of God in Rabbinic Literature," *Prooftexts* 12.2 (1992): 151–74; and in Kabbalah, see Gershom Scholem, *Major Trends in Jewish Mysticism,* 3rd ed. (New York: Schocken Books, 1954), esp. 63–67.

3. See, for instance, Jacob J. Finkelstein, "Bible and Babel," *Commentary* 26 (1958): 431–44, esp. 441.

4. See the introduction to my *Love & Joy: Law, Language, and Religion in*

Ancient Israel (New York: The Jewish Theological Seminary of America, 1992), esp. 5–6; cf. Stephen A. Geller, *Sacred Enigmas: Literary Religion in the Hebrew Bible* (New York: Routledge, 1996), 170, where he describes "the unique aspect of biblical religion"; and also his article, "The God of the Covenant," in *One God or Many? Concepts of Divinity in the Ancient World,* ed. Barbara N. Porter (Chebeague, Maine: Casco Bay Assyriological Institute, 2000), 273–319.

5. The greatest proponent of this viewpoint is Abraham J. Heschel, see Heschel, *Man Is Not Alone: A Philosophy of Religion* (New York: Farrar, Straus & Young, 1951); Heschel, *God in Search of Man: A Philosophy of Judaism* (Philadelphia: Jewish Publication Society of America, 1955); and Heschel, *The Prophets* (Philadelphia: Jewish Publication Society of America, 1962).

6. See Heschel, *The Prophets,* chs. 12–18. For a treatment of the divine personality of the biblical God from a literary-psychological point of view, see, for example, Richard E. Friedman, *The Hidden Face of God* (San Francisco: HarperCollins, 1995), originally published as *The Disappearance of God: A Divine Mystery* (Boston: Little, Brown, 1995); and Jack Miles, *God: A Biography* (New York: Alfred A. Knopf, 1995).

7. Erich Auerbach, *Mimesis: The Representation of Reality in Western Literature,* trans. Willard R. Trask (Princeton: Princeton University Press, 1953). Among the more recent works, see Robert Alter, *The Art of Biblical Narrative* (New York: Basic Books, 1981); Shimon Bar-Efrat, *Narrative Art in the Bible* (Sheffield, U.K.: Almond, 1989); Robert Polzin, *David and the Deuteronomist: A Literary Study of Deuteronomic History* (Bloomington: Indiana University Press, 1993); and Tikva Frymer-Kensky, *Reading the Women of the Bible* (New York: Schocken Books, 2002).

8. See *Love & Joy,* ch. 1 and "God and the World" in this volume.

9. Edmond La B. Cherbonnier, "The Logic of Biblical Anthropomorphism," *Harvard Theological Review* 55 (1962): 187–206; Heschel, *The Prophets,* chs. 16–17.

10. For example, see Gerhard von Rad, *Old Testament Theology,* 2 vols., trans. D. M. G. Stalker (New York: Harper & Row, 1965); and George Ernest Wright, *God Who Acts: Biblical Theology as Recital,* Studies in Biblical Theology 8 (London: SCM, 1952).

11. See the literature cited on the first page of William L. Moran's article, "The Ancient Near Eastern Background of the Love of God in Deuteronomy," *Catholic Biblical Quarterly* 25 (1963): 77–87. On *agape* and *eros,* see Anders Nygren, *Agape and Eros,* trans. Philip S. Watson (Philadelphia: Westminster, 1953).

12. See George E. Mendenhall, "Covenant Forms in Israelite Tradition," *Biblical Archaeologist* 17 (1954): 50–74, reprinted with

corrections in *Biblical Archaeologist Reader* 3 (1970): 25–53; Mendenhall, *The Tenth Generation: The Origins of the Biblical Tradition* (Baltimore: Johns Hopkins University Press, 1973); Moran, "The Ancient Near Eastern Background"; Moshe Weinfeld, "The Covenant of Grant in the Old Testament and in the Ancient Near East," *Journal of the American Oriental Society* 90 (1970): 184–203; Weinfeld, "Covenant Terminology in the Ancient Near East and Its Influence on the West," *Journal of the American Oriental Society* 93 (1973): 190–99; Weinfeld, *Deuteronomy and the Deuteronomic School* (Oxford: Clarendon, 1972; repr. Winona Lake, Ind.: Eisenbrauns, 1992); Weinfeld, "Covenant Making in Anatolia and Mesopotamia," *Journal of the Ancient Near Eastern Society* [*JANES*] 22 (1993): 135–39; and Hayim Tadmor, "Treaty and Oath in the Ancient Near East: A Historian's Approach," in *Humanizing America's Iconic Book,* ed. Gene M. Tucker and Douglas A. Knight (Chico, Calif.: Scholars, 1982), 127–52. For the history of scholarly discussion on this subject, see Robert A. Oden Jr., "The Place of Covenant in the Religion of Israel," in *Ancient Israelite Religion: Essays in Honor of Frank Moore Cross,* ed. Patrick D. Miller Jr. et al. (Philadelphia: Fortress, 1987), 429–47.

13. For the covenant and *Heilsgeschichte,* see Jon D. Levenson, "The Theologies of Commandment in Biblical Israel," *Harvard Theological Review* 73 (1980): 17–33.

14. See the discussion of prophetic intercession in *Love & Joy,* ch. 1.

15. On kinship and covenant in ancient Israel, see Frank Moore Cross, *From Epic to Canon: History and Literature in Ancient Israel* (Baltimore: Johns Hopkins University Press, 1998), 3–21. For God's earlier relationship with Abraham and the unconditional covenant, see Weinfeld, "The Covenant of Grant."

16. For the sacrifices God is ready to make for this creative urge, see *Love & Joy,* esp. 44–45.

Chapter 7: The Living Machine

1. *Tanhuma Buber, Toledot* 5 in *Midrash Tanhuma,* ed. Solomon Buber (Vilna: Roma, 1885), 128.

2. Zohar, *Naso', Sefer Ha-Zohar 'al Hamishah Humshe Torah,* 3 vols, ed. Reuven Margoliot (Jerusalem: Mosad Ha-rav Kuk, 1964), 3:129b.

Chapter 8: Divine Aspirations: Four Aspects of Kingship

1. Thorkild Jacobsen, *Toward the Image of Tammuz and Other Essays on Mesopotamian History and Culture,* esp. 73–103; and Jacobsen, *The Treasures of Darkness: A History of Mesopotamian Religion* (New Haven: Yale University Press, 1976). See my review on Jacobsen's *The Treasures of Darkness* in *Love & Joy,* ch. 3.

2. See *Love & Joy,* ch. 3.

3. See also Exodus 10:1–2.

4. For more on this, see *Love & Joy,* ch. 2.

5. For example, "The Bible tells us nothing about God in Himself; all its sayings refer to His relation to man. His own life and essence are neither told nor disclosed. We hear of no reflexive concern, of no passions, except a passion for justice. The only events in the life of God the Bible knows of are acts done for the sake of man." (Heschel, *Man Is Not Alone,* 143–44). See also his *God in Search of Man,* and *The Prophets.*

6. The bear may eat at 3:00, the lion at 10:00, the peacock at 4:00, and so on. Cf. *Tanhuma, Noah* 9, where we have a midrash about how Noah learned from his Creator when and what to feed each animal in that floating hotel of the deluge.

7. A similar idea is found in ancient Egyptian literature. See John A. Wilson, trans., "A Hymn to Amon-Re," in *ANET,* 366.

8. Tablet XI. See E. A. Speiser's translation in *ANET,* 93.

9. On the arts of divination in Mesopotamia, see A. Leo Oppenheim, *Ancient Mesopotamia: Portrait of a Dead Civilization* (Chicago: University of Chicago Press, 1964), 206–27.

10. See, for instance, Oppenheim, *Ancient Mesopotamia,* 226–27; and Henri Frankfort, *Kingship and the God: A Study of Ancient Near Eastern Religion as the Integration of Society & Nature* (Chicago: University of Chicago Press, 1948), 251–61.

11. Read: *'k* not *'yk,* following Arnold B. Ehrilch, *Randglossen zur Hebräischen Bibel,* 7 vols. (Leipzig: Hinrichs, 1908–14), 4:246.

12. *'shytk bbnym,* "to place in sonship/sons"; cf. H. L. Ginsberg, "Studies in Hosea 1–3," *Yehezkel Kaufmann Jubilee Volume,* ed. Menahem Haran (Jerusalem: Magnes, 1960), 51–52 n. 4; Ginsberg, "Ugaritico-Phoenica," *JANES* 5 (1973):138.

13. Cf. Moshe Weinfeld, "'You Will Find Favour ... in the Sight of God and Man' (Proverbs 3:4): The History of an Idea," *Eretz-Israel* 16 (1982): 93–99 [in Hebrew].

14. David Weiss Halivni, *Midrash, Mishnah, and Gemara: The Jewish Prediction for Justified Law* (Cambridge, Mass.: Harvard University Press, 1986).

15. Ibid., 5–6.

16. Cf. Franz Rosenthal's translation in *ANET,* 654–55.

17. Ibid., 654.

18. See Jonah C. Greenfield, "Notes on the Asitawada (Karatepe) Inscription," *Eretz-Israel* 14 (1978): 74–77 [in Hebrew]; and Moshe Weinfeld, "Justice and Righteousness as the Task of the King," in *Social Justice in Ancient Israel and in the Ancient Near East* (Minneapolis: Fortress Press, 1995), 45–56.

19. Kaufmann, *Toledot,* 5:711–27; cf. 5:433–47.

20. For further details, see Weinfeld's *Social Justice*.

Chapter 9: Power, Love, and Justice: The Positive Expression of the Divine Will

1. This insight occurred to me when I came upon the title of Tillich's book *Love, Power, and Justice: Ontological Analyses and Ethical Applications* (New York: Oxford University Press, 1954).
2. Kaufmann, *Toledot,* and Kaufmann, *Religion of Israel.*
3. Heschel, *God in Search of Man;* Heschel, *The Prophets;* and Maisels, *Mahshavah ve-'Emet.* See also my *Love & Joy* and my other essays in this volume.
4. See E. A. Speiser, "Authority and Law in Mesopotamia," in *Oriental and Biblical Studies: Collected Writings of E. A. Speiser,* ed. J. J. Finkelstein and Moshe Greenberg (Philadelphia: University of Pennsylvania Press, 1967), 313–23, and also other essays in that collection.
5. See my *Love & Joy,* 40–41.

Chapter 10: On the Uses of Divine Power

1. See my book *Love & Joy,* 44–46.

Chapter 11: Image and Imagination in the Bible

1. Cf. *Tanhuma, Ki Tissa'* 22; *Exodus Rabbah* 43:6.

Chapter 14: Intent, Volition, and the Roots of Rabbinic Prayer

1. *Berakhot* 5:1.
2. *Seder Tefillat Shabbat* in *Seder Rav 'Amram,* ed. Daniel Goldschmidt (Jerusalem: Mosad Harav Kuk, 1971), 63.
3. *Seder Birkot ha-Shahar* in *Seder Rav 'Amram,* 3.
4. *Seder Qeriat Shema' Uvirkhotehah* in *Seder Rav 'Amram,* 14. It is interesting to note in passing that very similar passages appear in Muslim prayers designed to help in the memorization of the entire Qur'an. I will quote one in full, as it appears in Constance E. Padwick, *Muslim Devotions: A Study of Prayer-Manuals in Common Use* (London: SPCK, 1961), 114:

   I ask Thee O God by Thy Majesty and the Light of Thy Countenance to bind to my heart the memorizing of Thy Book as Thou hast taught me, and to endow me with the (power of) reciting it with the grammatical inflection that shall win me Thy approval. And I ask Thee to illuminate my heart and my vision through Thy Book, and to grant my tongue fluency in it, and to relieve my heart and dilate my breast and wash away my sins by means, and (I ask) that Thou wilt strengthen me for this and help me in it, for none can help me and aid me to the truth but Thyself.

(Recite this prayer for three weeks or five or seven, and you will memorize it with God's permission).

Padwick's source is 'Aṣ-Ṣuyūtī's *al-Ḥirzu 'l-manī,* 125.

5. C. J. Gadd published the text of the inscription in his article "The Harran Inscription of Nabonidus," *Anatolian Studies* VIII (1958): 35–92. Our translation is taken from A. Leo Oppenheim, trans., "The Mother of Nabonidus" in *ANET,* 561.

6. Oppenheim, *ANET,* 563.

7. Ibid.

8. The text may be found in Stephen Langdon, *Die neubabylonischen Königsinschriften,* trans. Rudolf Zehnpfund, *Vorderasiatische Bibliothek* 4 (Leipzig: J. C. Hinrichs, 1912) [*VAB* IV], 122–23, lines 57–72. Our translation is from Thorkild Jacobsen's *Treasures of Darkness,* 238–39. It would be relevant to quote here Professor Jacobsen's complete remarks concerning the prayer:

The application of quietistic piety to war—often to ruthless and cruel war—is of course an extreme. In the peaceful aspects of life it showed to greater advantage, enhancing such truly religious attitudes as sincere humility before the divine and trust, not only in miraculous assistance and intervention, but in greater divine wisdom. In that respect it may perhaps be considered the only real religious insight that can be credited to the first millennium in Mesopotamia. As we find it around the middle of the millennium in inscriptions of Neo-Babylonian rulers it seems, however, less a part of Mesopotamian religious tradition than a new impulse from the simple piety of the Aramean tribesmen to whom the Neo-Babylonian rulers traced their lineage. Similarly, the noble faith of the Achaemenids who followed them was a new impulse with its roots in the belief of Iranian herdsmen. To illustrate this new, foreign, Neo-Babylonian piety in its most attractive form, we may quote a prayer to Marduk by Nebuchadnezer of the early sixth century B.C., thus bringing our consideration of ancient Mesopotamian religion to a positive conclusion (page 238).

9. *VAB* IV, 76–77, col. II, lines 54–55 and col. III, lines 1–4. Our translation is based on the English predecessor to *VAB* IV, Stephen Langdon, *Building Inscriptions of the Neo-Babylonian Empire* (Paris: E. Leroux, 1905), 67. Also compare *VAB* IV, page 110, col. III, lines 7–11; and Langdon, 109.

10. *VAB* IV, 98–99, col. I, lines 27–32 and col. II, lines 1–5; Langdon, 95.

11. *VAB* IV, 100–101, col. II, lines 17–18, Langdon, 95.

12. *VAB* IV, 154–156, col. V, lines 4–10; and see Langdon, 159, but his translation is too fragmentary to be of much help.

13. *VAB* IV, 62–63, col. II, lines 14–22; Langdon, 51.

14. These dates and those brought above are from J. A. Brinkman's

"Mesopotamian Chronology of the Historical Period," published as an appendix to A. Leo Oppenheim, *Ancient Mesopotamia: Portrait of a Dead Civilization* (Chicago: University of Chicago Press, 1977), 335–52.

15. *VAB* IV, 238–39, col. II, lines 39–40. I have been unable to obtain the second part of Langdon's work, which contains the Nabonidus inscriptions.

16. *VAB* IV, 240–41, col. III, lines 20–22.

17. *VAB* IV, 250–51, col. III, lines 54–55.

18. *VAB* IV, 252–53, col. II, lines 13–15.

19. *VAB* IV, 252–53, col. II, lines 19–31.

20. Jacob Licht, *Megillat ha-Hodayot* (Jerusalem: Bialik Institute, 1957), 31, 38.

21. Ibid., 39.

22. *Serakhim (= Megillat Ha-Serakhim)*, VI, line 14 in Jacob Licht, *Megillat Ha-Serakhim* (Jerusalem: Bialik Institute, 1965), 149.

23. *The Jewish War*, Book II, para. 120.

24. *War Scroll*, VII, line 5 in Yigael Yadin, *The Scroll of The War of the Sons of Light against the Sons of Darkness* (Jerusalem: Bialik Institute, 1957), 300.

25. *War Scroll*, X, line 5 in Yadin, 316.

26. *Siḥu* in the sense of declaration, see Psalm 105:2.

27. *Hodayot (= Megillat ha-Hodayot)*, I, lines 35–37, in Licht, 63–64.

28. *Hodayot*, II, lines 17–18, in Licht, 68; cf. XIII, line 19, in Licht, 184, and also XIV, line 8, in Licht, 188.

29. A pun: the community itself was called a *yaḥad*, the word for "unison."

30. *Hodayot*, III, line 23, in Licht, 84.

31. *Hodayot*, VI, line 31, in Licht, 96.

32. *Hodayot*, IX, line 16, in Licht, 145.

33. *Hodayot*, XII, lines 22–23, in Licht, 176.

34. *Hodayot*, X, line 27, in Licht, 157, but see the text in A. M. Habermann, *Megilloth Midbar Yehudah* (Tel Aviv: Machbaroth Lesifrut Publishing House, 1957), 126. The Qumran community commonly referred to itself as "the servants" or "the sons of the servants."

35. *Hodayot*, XI, line 9, in Licht, 162.

36. *Hodayot*, XII, line 13, in Licht, 175, assuming *raz = sod* in the context.

37. *Hodayot*, XIV, lines 25–27, in Licht, 192–93. The point is that membership in the community was by free choice. Here the poet thanks God for enlightening him to see the just path. But cf. *Hodayot*, XV, line 23, in Licht, 198, where the poet declares that he desired *('aviti)* to enter the community. Still, the context suggests that God inspired that will in him. Also, cf. *Hodayot*, XVI, line 10,

in Licht, 203, where the poet says that he chose to do God's will *(baḥarti);* but this is in a liturgical context, where it is clear that the poet means to thank God for causing the choice. At any rate, elsewhere, for example, *Hodayot,* XVII, line 14, in Licht, 208, the same verb is used to say that God chooses His own worshippers. The members of the community are also said to have been chosen by God in *War Scroll,* XII, line 1, in Yadin, 326.

Chapter 15: Joy in the Liturgy

1. *Mechilta d'Rabbi Ismael,* ed. Hayyim S. Horowitz and Israel A. Rabin (Frankfurt am Main: Kauffmann, 1931), Jethro, ch. 2, page 208.
2. Ibid., page 210.
3. Ibid., ch. 4, page 218.
4. Ibid., ch. 2, page 209.
5. Ibid., ch. 5, page 219.
6. *Tanna de-Be Eliyahu* (Ish Shalom), ch. 17, page 83.
7. *Seder Rav 'Amram,* ed. Daniel Goldschmidt (Jerusalem: Mosad Harav Kuk, 1971), 52.
8. See S. Lieberman, "Mishnat Shir ha-Shirim," in Gershom G. Scholem, *Jewish Gnosticism, Merkabah Mysticism and Talmudic Tradition,* 2nd ed. (New York: The Jewish Theological Seminary of America, 1965), 118–26.
9. See Gershom G. Scholem, "The Age of Shiur Komah Speculation and a Passage in Origen," in *Jewish Gnosticism,* 36–42.
10. Seligmann Baer, *Seder 'Avodat Israel* (Rödelheim, Ger.: I. Lehrberger, 1868), 78. The word *u-mamlikim* is missing in *Seder Rav 'Amram.*
11. Ibid., 185.
12. *B. Berakhot* 13b, with specific reference to Rabbi Judah the Patriarch.
13. *M. Tamid* 5:1.
14. Dov Jarden, *The Liturgical Poetry of Rabbi Solomon Ibn Gabirol,* 2 vols. (Jerusalem: Akademiyah ha-Amerikanit le-mad'ae ha-Yahadut, 1971–72), 1:283–84.
15. *Siddur R. Saadija Gaon,* ed. Israel Davidson et al. (Jerusalem: Mekize Nidramim, 1941), page 273, lines 198 and 209; see page 275, line 247, for the same idea expressed by the verb *takaf* from the word *tekef,* immediate.
16. Ibid., page 279, lines 73, 77, and 81.
17. Ibid., page 277, lines 31–32.
18. Ibid., page 277, line 41.
19. Ibid., page 270, lines 137–38.
20. Cf. *M. Yoma* 2:2.
21. Daniel Goldschmidt, *Mahzor le-Yamim Ha-Nora'im,* 2 vols.

(Jersualem: Koren, 1970), 2:439, line 33.

22. *Siddur R. Saadija Gaon,* page 271, line 152.

23. Goldschmidt, *Mahzor le-Yamim Ha-Nora'im,* 2:443, lines 57 and 59. For running as a metaphor for willingness to perform, see *M. Abot* 5:20; *Avot de-Rabbi Natan,* ed. Solomon Schechter (Vienna: Ch. D. Lippe, 1887), text A, ch. 41, page 133; *Tosefta Sotah* 4:1 in *The Tosefta: The Order of Nashim,* ed. Saul Lieberman (New York: The Jewish Theological Seminary of America, 1973), 167. See also *Midrash Tanhuma (Buber)* to Genesis 18:2–7 in *Midrash Tanhuma: Ein agadischer commentar zum Pentateuch von Rabbi Tanchuma ben Rabbi Abba,* ed. Solomon Buber (Vilna: Itzkowski, 1885), *Va-yera'* 5, 86–87; cf. also the *Targum* to Habakkuk 2:2 in light of *Onqelos* to Exodus 10:16.

24. Goldschmidt, *Mahzor le-Yamim Ha-Nora'im,* 2:445, line 72.

25. Ibid.

26. Job 41:14.

27. Goldschmidt, *Mahzor le-Yamim Ha-Nora'im,* 2:451, line 52.

28. Ibid., 2:457, line 114.

29. Ibid., 2:451, line 51.

30. Ibid., 2:458, line 125.

31. Ibid., 2:459, line 135.

32. Ibid., 2:459, line 141.

33. Ibid., 2:455, line 89 and 2:461, line 154.

34. Ibid., 2:460, line 152.

35. Ibid.

36. Ibid., 2:460, line 148.

37. Ibid., 2:460, line 151. Yannai also used the word *daṣ* in his description of the service in the expression *daṣim le-ṭaharah.* He also makes use of the verb *gahaṣ* in the same sense in the expression *gohaṣim be-zrizut be-kol 'avodat qodesh;* see Saul Lieberman, "Hazzanut Yannai," *Sinai* 4 (1939): 226; and Menahem Zulay, *Piyyutei Yannai* (Berlin: Schoken, 1938), 159. For the parallel usage of *samah* and *gahaṣ,* see *Genesis Rabbah* 39:8, with the variant readings in *Midrasch Bereschit Rabba mit kritischem apparat und kommentar,* ed. Julius Theodor and Chanoch Albeck (Berlin: Itzkowski, 1903–29), 371, line 6; cf. also "II *g-h-ṣ,*" *Aruch Completum,* ed. Alexander Kohut, 9 vols. (New York: Pardes, 1955), 2:252.

38. Goldschmidt, *Mahzor le-Yamim Ha-Nora'im,* 2:457, line 118.

Chapter 16: Love and Alacrity in Other Liturgies

1. Solomon Schechter, "Genizah Specimens," *Jewish Quarterly Review: The Original Series* 10 (1898): 654ff. This benediction seems to have vanished from the liturgy; see Abudraham's *Perush ha-berakhot veha-tefilot Abudarham Ha-shalem* (Jerusalem: Usha,

1963), 80: "and the reason for which we do not say the blessing ... on the reading of the Shema', like we do for other commandments." But part of the blessing may have survived in a prayer preserved in the *Mahzor B'nei Romi*.

2. Ibid., 655, and cf. Jacob Mann, "Genizah Fragments of the Palestinian Order of the Service," *Hebrew Union College Annual* 2 (1925): 287, n. 51.

3. *Y. Berakhot* 4:2, 7d.

4. *M. Abot* 2:9.

5. *Seder Rav 'Amram*, 63.

6. *Y. Berakhot* 4:2, 7d.

7. *B. Berakhot* 17a.

8. *Dikduke Sofrim*, ad loc.

9. *Seder Rav 'Amram*, 79.

10. Ibid., 78; see the phrase *u-naqriv lefanekha be-'ahavah* in the Sabbath Rosh Hodesh prayer, ibid., 90.

11. Ibid., 47 (see the apparatus below).

12. *B. Sanhedrin* 42a.

13. Frank E. Brightman, *Liturgies Eastern and Western* (Oxford: Clarendon, 1896), 79.

14. P. Kuvochinsky, *The Divine Liturgy of the Holy Orthodox Catholic Apostolic Greco-Russian Church* (London: Cape and Fenwick, 1909), 67–68.

15. Ibid., 81.

16. It is certainly no less significant to note that it was not only in a liturgical context that the sects of ancient Christianity worked within the metaphorical context which we have established. In fact, perhaps the most eloquent statement of the far-reaching implications of the metaphor to explain the human condition is found in a prose work, *The Book of the Laws of Countries*, composed by Philip, the disciple of Bardaisan, the "giant of Edessan literature." Judah B. Segal, *Edessa "The Blessed City"* (Oxford: Clarendon, 1970), 35.

Chapter 17: The Priestly Benediction

1. See *b. Sotah* 39–39b; I thank Prof. David Rosenthal for this reference.

2. See *Numbers Rabbah*, 11:2, although there it is the Israelites who denigrate the value of the blessing.

3. *Numbers Rabbah*, 11:2.

4. *Midrash Tanhuma, Ve-zo't Ha-berakhah*, ch. 1.

5. *Midrash Tanhuma, 'Aharei Mot*, ch. 12.

6. A. A. Halevi, *'Olamah shel Ha-aggadah* (Tel Aviv: Dvir, 1972), 30. Similarly, from a Greek source we learn that when Poseidon and Apollo built the walls of Troy, they included two mortals in the

work, since it was fated that the walls of Troy were to be destroyed. It was of utmost importance that humans take part in the building, for if they did not it would never be possible otherwise for Troy to be destroyed.

7. *Numbers Rabbah,* 11:2.
8. *Midrash Tanhuma, Naso',* ch. 18.
9. *Sifre Zuta* to Numbers 6:27; cf. *Sifre Zuta,* ed. H. S. Horovitz (Lodz: Masorah), 250; cf. *Midrash Ha-Gadol: Bamidbar,* ed. Tsevi M. Rabinowitz (Jerusalem: Mosad Harav Kook, 1967), 101, and *Numbers Rabbah* 11:8.
10. *Tanhuma (Buber) Naso',* 18 in *Midrash Tanhuma,* ed. Solomon Buber (Vilna: Roma, 1885), 34, and see *Numbers Rabbah,* 11:4. Rashi, commenting on Numbers 6:23, quotes this midrash, but substitutes *ḥipazon* (speed) for *angaria* (duress). Rashi to Numbers 6:23, in *Raschii (Salomonis Isaacidis)* in *Pentateuchum Commentarius,* ed. Abraham Berliner (Berlin: Sumptibus Editoris, 1866), 251.
11. *Numbers Rabbah* 11:4.
12. See Zohar, *Naso',* the passage begins, *"Vesamu et shmi,"* in *Sefer Ha-Zohar 'al Hamishah Humshe Torah,* ed. Reuven Margoliot, 3 vols. (Jerusalem: Mosad Harav Kuk, 1964), 3:147b.

Chapter 18: God and the World

1. Thus, for example, nomistic Judaism had room not merely for what Kadushin has called "normal mysticism" but for all sorts of truly mystical phenomena, from the vision of the divine body and the hearing of the angelic chorus to the Gnosticism of Lurianic Kabbalah and its antinomian transmutation in Sabbatianism. It had room for the positive attitude toward sexuality found in many rabbinic statements as well as the morbid attitude found in many medieval pietistic works and in Hasidism (cf. Abraham Joshua Heschel, *Kotsk: The Struggle for Integrity,* 2 vols. [Tel Aviv: Hamenora, 1973]). It had room for an aristocratic piety based on the centrality of learning as well as a more popular piety based on the adoration of the charismatic leader and his theurgic powers.
2. While Judaism, unlike Gnosticism, does not see the world as evil, at least one of the biblical sources (Gen. 8:21) does see man as such. The realistic optimism that has been presented above is but one strand in biblical thinking. Clearly, Jeremiah's vision of the new heart (Jer. 31:31ff.) represents a divine loss of nerve concerning man's educability. God no longer believes that man can be taught to be good under the guidance of the Torah. Yet, in spite of His exasperation with the old educational dispensation—the belief that man can independently assimilate the message being taught—God keeps trying new methods. If older methods based on freedom do

not work, a kind of "Skinnerian programming" is contemplated. God will write the Torah, not on books but directly on the heart. So programmed, the "pretaped heart" should automatically lead man to performance of the commandments and thus to the ultimate felicity in which it will no longer be necessary for men to teach each other the word of God, for it will have become instinctive.

To cite a modern example, it was Heschel himself, whose whole corpus of writing breathed a positive, optimistic, almost humanistic spirit, who spent the last year of his life investigating the life and teachings of the Kotzker Rebbe, a morbid, relentlessly honest investigator of man's sinfulness and a passionate hater of the world and worldliness. One of the first lectures Heschel gave upon arriving in America was his Yiddish "Kotzk and Kierkegaard," which finally took shape in English as *A Passion for Truth* (New York: Farrar, Straus & Giroux, 1973).

A friend of mine, upon leaving a famous East European yeshiva, was given the following parting blessing by his former teacher: "Sir, I know from now on you will not be a good Jew; I also know that having been with us, you will never fully enjoy the fleshly pleasures of the world."

3. Cf. Gershom Scholem, *Major Trends in Jewish Mysticism,* 3rd ed. (New York: Schocken Books, 1954); and Hans Jonas, *Gnostic Religion: The Message of the Alien God and the Beginnings of Christianity,* 2nd ed. (Boston: Beacon, 1963).

4. For better or for worse, much of my understanding of Christianity has been influenced by Kierkegaard and, especially, by Anders Nygren's *Agape and Eros,* trans. Philip S. Watson (Philadelphia: Westminster, 1953). My presentation may thus not do justice to more Catholic positions, which, in their stress on natural law, may be less extreme and relatively more viable. Furthermore, contemporary Christianity's understandable but violent repudiation of its traditional resentment against the world and worldliness is hardly reflected in the above statement. The author may more correctly reflect the tradition against which many modernists are reacting, rather than Christianity as it is actually lived, with its new appreciation of the world of the senses and its new concern with the world of communal responsibility.

Chapter 19: A Jewish View of God's Relation to the World

1. Freely adapted from the Babylonian Talmud, *Sanhedrin* 38b. While the ontological reality of angels in rabbinic literature cannot be totally denied, more often than not, angels seem to be used as nothing more than literary devices, dramatic projections of one of two opposing moods in the conflicted divine mind. Thus, in our

midrash, God "plays out" divine love, and the angels externalize the opposing mood of God: divine anger or realism. Furthermore, the rather abstract value concepts of *din* (strict judgment) and *raḥamim* (mercy) find a more dramatic, and pedagogically more effective, expression and concretization.

2. Cf. *Genesis Rabbah* 9:7. This and all subsequent citations from the midrashic literature are free renditions rather than literal translations.
3. Cf. Babylonian Talmud, *Yoma* 60b. For more literature, cf. Ephraim E. Urbach, *The Sages: Their Concepts and Beliefs*, 2 vols., trans. Israel Abrahams (Jerusalem: Magnes, 1975), 2:895, n. 24.
4. *Tanhuma, Bere'shit* 7ff.
5. *Genesis Rabbah* 9:5. For more details, cf. Urbach, *The Sages*, 1:420ff.
6. Cf. E. A. Speiser's translation of the Gilgamesh epic in James B. Pritchard, ed., *ANET*, 72ff.
7. Cf. Yitzhak Heinemann, *Darkhe ha-Aggadah* (Jerusalem: Magnes, 1949–50), 49ff.
8. The author will be forgiven the poetic license of fusing elements derived from different midrashim all dealing with the same theme: the divine workday after the six days of creation. The themes of divine study and judging/administering are found in the Babylonian Talmud, *Avodah Zarah* 3b.
9. The theme of the divine matchmaker is found in *Genesis Rabbah* 68:4 and in many other places.

Chapter 20: Judaism and Secular Culture

1. Saul Lieberman, *Greek in Jewish Palestine: Studies in the Life and Manners of Jewish Palestine in the II-IV Centuries C.E.* (New York: The Jewish Theological Seminary of America: 1942); and Lieberman, *Hellenism in Jewish Palestine: Studies in the Literary Transmission, Beliefs and Manners of Palestine in the I Century B.C.E.–IV Century C.E.* (New York: The Jewish Theological Seminary of America: 1950).

Chapter 21: On the Demythologizing of Religion

1. John Dewey, *A Common Faith* (New Haven, Conn.: Yale University Press, 1934).

CREDITS

The following essays have been previously published in slightly different form.

"Biblical Anthropomorphism" will appear in the Stephen A. Geller Festschrift (forthcoming from Eisenbrauns).

"God and the World" and "A Jewish View of God's Relation to the World" originally appeared under the title, "God and the World: A Jewish View," in *The Samuel Friedland Lectures* 1967–1974 (New York: Jewish Theological Seminary of America, 1974), 63–84.

"Theology and Poetics" originally appeared in *Conservative Judaism* 51 (1998): 3–9.

"Toward a Phenomenology of the Senses" originally appeared in Deborah Rosenthal, *Eve's Vocabulary: Paintings 1988–1998* (Hebrew Union College–Jewish Institute of Religion: New York, 1999), 13–17.

"On the Demythologizing of Religion" originally appeared under the title, "Dewey on Religion: An Introduction," in *Conservative Judaism* 30 (1976): 40–43.

INDEX

INDEX OF JEWISH SOURCES

Entries in italics are citations listed in extracts from other works.

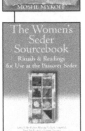

Theology/Philosophy

Judaism, Physics and God: Searching for Sacred Metaphors in a Post-Einstein World
By Rabbi David W. Nelson
In clear, non-technical terms, this provocative fusion of religion and science examines the great theories of modern physics to find new ways for contemporary people to express their spiritual beliefs and thoughts.
6 x 9, 352 pp, Hardcover, ISBN 1-58023-252-3 **$24.99**

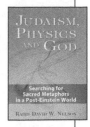

Aspects of Rabbinic Theology
By Solomon Schechter. New Introduction by Dr. Neil Gillman.
6 x 9, 448 pp, Quality PB, ISBN 1-879045-24-9 **$19.95**

Broken Tablets: Restoring the Ten Commandments and Ourselves
Edited by Rachel S. Mikva. Introduction by Lawrence Kushner. Afterword by Arnold Jacob Wolf.
6 x 9, 192 pp, Quality PB, ISBN 1-58023-158-6 **$16.95**; Hardcover, ISBN 1-58023-066-0 **$21.95**

Creating an Ethical Jewish Life
A Practical Introduction to Classic Teachings on How to Be a Jew
By Dr. Byron L. Sherwin and Seymour J. Cohen
6 x 9, 336 pp, Quality PB, ISBN 1-58023-114-4 **$19.95**

The Death of Death: Resurrection and Immortality in Jewish Thought
By Dr. Neil Gillman 6 x 9, 336 pp, Quality PB, ISBN 1-58023-081-4 **$18.95**

Evolving Halakhah: A Progressive Approach to Traditional Jewish Law
By Rabbi Dr. Moshe Zemer
6 x 9, 480 pp, Quality PB, ISBN 1-58023-127-6 **$29.95**; Hardcover, ISBN 1-58023-002-4 **$40.00**

Hasidic Tales: Annotated & Explained
By Rabbi Rami Shapiro. Foreword by Andrew Harvey, SkyLight Illuminations series editor.
5½ x 8½, 240 pp, Quality PB, ISBN 1-893361-86-1 **$16.95** *(A SkyLight Paths Book)*

A Heart of Many Rooms: Celebrating the Many Voices within Judaism
By Dr. David Hartman 6 x 9, 352 pp, Quality PB, ISBN 1-58023-156-X **$19.95**

The Hebrew Prophets: Selections Annotated & Explained
Translation & Annotation by Rabbi Rami Shapiro. Foreword by Zalman M. Schachter-Shalomi
5½ x 8½, 224 pp, Quality PB, ISBN 1-59473-037-7 **$16.99** *(A SkyLight Paths book)*

I Am Jewish: Personal Reflections Inspired by the Last Words of Daniel Pearl
Edited by Judea and Ruth Pearl
6 x 9, 304 pp, Deluxe PB w/flaps, ISBN 1-58023-259-0 **$18.99**
Hardcover, ISBN 1-58023-183-7 **$24.99**

Keeping Faith with the Psalms: Deepen Your Relationship with God Using the Book of Psalms *By Daniel F. Polish* 6 x 9, 272 pp, Hardcover, ISBN 1-58023-179-9 **$24.95**

The Last Trial
On the Legends and Lore of the Command to Abraham to Offer Isaac as a Sacrifice
By Shalom Spiegel. New Introduction by Judah Goldin.
6 x 9, 208 pp, Quality PB, ISBN 1-879045-29-X **$18.95**

A Living Covenant: The Innovative Spirit in Traditional Judaism
By Dr. David Hartman 6 x 9, 368 pp, Quality PB, ISBN 1-58023-011-3 **$18.95**

Love and Terror in the God Encounter
The Theological Legacy of Rabbi Joseph B. Soloveitchik
By Dr. David Hartman
6 x 9, 240 pp, Quality PB, ISBN 1-58023-176-4 **$19.95**; Hardcover, ISBN 1-58023-112-8 **$25.00**

Seeking the Path to Life
Theological Meditations on God and the Nature of People, Love, Life and Death
By Rabbi Ira F. Stone 6 x 9, 160 pp, Quality PB, ISBN 1-879045-47-8 **$14.95**

The Spirit of Renewal: Finding Faith after the Holocaust
By Rabbi Edward Feld 6 x 9, 224 pp, Quality PB, ISBN 1-879045-40-0 **$16.95**

Tormented Master: *The Life and Spiritual Quest of Rabbi Nahman of Bratslav*
By Dr. Arthur Green 6 x 9, 416 pp, Quality PB, ISBN 1-879045-11-7 **$19.99**

Your Word Is Fire: The Hasidic Masters on Contemplative Prayer
Edited and translated by Dr. Arthur Green and Barry W. Holtz
6 x 9, 160 pp, Quality PB, ISBN 1-879045-25-7 **$15.95**

About Jewish Lights

People of all faiths and backgrounds yearn for books that attract, engage, educate, and spiritually inspire.

Our principal goal is to stimulate thought and help all people learn about who the Jewish People are, where they come from, and what the future can be made to hold. While people of our diverse Jewish heritage are the primary audience, our books speak to people in the Christian world as well and will broaden their understanding of Judaism and the roots of their own faith.

We bring to you authors who are at the forefront of spiritual thought and experience. While each has something different to say, they all say it in a voice that you can hear.

Our books are designed to welcome you and then to engage, stimulate, and inspire. We judge our success not only by whether or not our books are beautiful and commercially successful, but by whether or not they make a difference in your life.

For your information and convenience, at the back of this book we have provided a list of other Jewish Lights books you might find interesting and useful. They cover all the categories of your life:

Bar/Bat Mitzvah
Bible Study / Midrash
Children's Books
Congregation Resources
Current Events / History
Ecology
Fiction: Mystery, Science Fiction
Grief / Healing
Holidays / Holy Days
Inspiration
Kabbalah / Mysticism / Enneagram

Life Cycle
Meditation
Parenting
Prayer
Ritual / Sacred Practice
Spirituality
Theology / Philosophy
Travel
Twelve Steps
Women's Interest

Stuart M. Matlins, Publisher

Or phone, mail or e-mail to: **JEWISH LIGHTS Publishing**
An imprint of Turner Publishing Company
4507 Charlotte Avenue • Suite 100 • Nashville, TN 37209
Tel: (615) 255-2665 • www.jewishlights.com
Prices subject to change.

For more information about each book, visit our website at www.jewishlights.com

Printed in the USA
CPSIA information can be obtained
at www.ICGtesting.com
JSHW022324140824
68134JS00019B/1280